LEARNING TO HEAR

---•---

THE
WHISPERS
OF GOD

---•---

D1468644

LEARNING TO HEAR

THE WHISPERS OF GOD

DONNA FITZPATRICK

WINEPRESS WP PUBLISHING

ISBN 1-57921-348-0
Library of Congress Catalog Card Number: 00-110893

To my husband, Dan, and to each of my children, who eagerly anticipated the arrival of this book. Because of their willing investment in me, it has truly become theirs.

. . . the Lord was not in the wind;

. . . the Lord was not in the earthquake;

. . . the Lord was not in the fire:

. . . after the fire came a

gentle whisper.

—1 Kings 19:11, 12 (NIV)

Contents

Acknowledgments

NEVER HAVE I EXPERIENCED THE PRIVILEGE OF SO MANY VARIED PEOPLE WORKING together to complete a project. To these people I owe great thanks and deep respect for their faithfulness—to me, and to the book you now hold in your hands. First, I thank my husband, Dan, for never tiring of "hearing" my latest version and for his valuable advice and insight. More importantly, for his undying devotion as a husband and his help to accomplish what I believe God placed in my heart to do—without which I would never have completed the first paragraph here.

Next I want to thank my sister, Irene Norris, who gave the gift of encouragement a new and beautiful meaning to me. Cecil Ringgenberg's experience in writing and editing was a true godsend, as well as Barbara Robidoux's help and encouraging sense of humor.

To the many friends (and my children) who let me tell their various "whisper" stories—*thank you!*

One other thanks—to the pastors who have influenced my life through the years: Pastor Merlin R. & Mary Carothers, Pastor Coleman & Mary Phillips, Rev. Billy & Betty Falling, Pastor George & Jean Simmons, Pastor Rick & Linda Hoskins, Pastor Jerome & Linda Andrews, Pastor Craig & Dianne Andrus, and Pastor Bill & Clara Bolin . . . *thank you for your faithfulness to His sheep!*

ONE
Listening As a Child

As a little child I listen.
Am I too small to hear?
Be still, My child, and listen.
He whispers very near.

KEVIN SHIFTED FROM ONE FOOT TO THE OTHER IN THE DOORWAY OF MY ROOM while his gaze roamed the walls in search of words. The book in my lap fell aside; my easygoing teen had seized my full attention. Sitting up straighter, I watched and waited until at last his eyes met mine, and he softly asked, "Mom . . . how do you know when God is talking to you?"

I relaxed back to my former position and smiled at my son. *Whew! Is that all?* I thought to myself. Then, of course, the magnitude of that question hit me! Perplexing questions are common in raising children, but I sometimes think I get more than my fair share in raising eight! How could I possibly answer my son's question, which reflects the inborn yearning of every heart? I sat pondering for a few minutes knowing I'd heard this question before—but never from one of my own children. Yet the Lord knows just what to do to prompt us to prayer.

I sought God for an answer I could give my son and all those who desire to hear His voice. After diligently seeking the Lord for insight on this, I discovered how to encourage the believer in hearing and recognizing His voice. *Learning to Hear the Whispers of God* is broken into three parts. The first part *establishes* that God does speak, the second part *encourages* the believer to hear; and the third part *explains* more about the whispers.

We begin the first part in learning to hear the whispers of God by *establishing* that our Lord *does* speak to His children . . .

God Speaks to His Children

Pulling the covers tighter to my chin, I closed my eyes—pretending not to see the morning light. Just then the bedroom door flew open as Abigail ran through it, jumped on the bed beside me and wiggled her little cherubic body inside the covers.

"Good morning, Mommy!" Abigail sing-songed as she placed her face as close as she could to mine. Opening one eye I said, "Go make Mommy some coffee, Abby." Opening both eyes, I watched to see her response.

Abigail smiled and said, "Sure." Then she sat up very still for a moment before turning toward me again. "Mommy," she said with a wrinkled up nose and the serious voice of a three-year-old, "I can't. I too little!"

Of course Abigail was too little to get me coffee, but reflecting upon that precious moment I know the Lord used her to whisper into my heart. We believers respond much the same way when it comes to hearing God's voice. We think we're too little, and certainly not like the spiritual giants who hear and walk in great faith. But does it really take a spiritual giant of great faith to hear God's whispers? No! God does not play with us the way I played with

Abigail. He doesn't ask us to do something we cannot do. Jesus said: "My sheep hear My voice, and I know them, and they follow Me" (John 10:27).

We *can* hear His voice because God *does* speak to His children. But how can we recognize God's voice? This takes us to the second part in learning to hear the Spirit's whispers by *encouraging* the believer to hear. Each of the following chapters contains stories of times when God whispered—"whisper stories." These whisper stories show the variety of ways the Lord may use to speak into our hearts and encourage us to recognize His voice. An extra benefit of reading these "whisper stories" is that, in every case, God used them to teach a basic truth contained in His Word. Each story helps us in both understanding and remembering that truth. It's a fun way to learn biblical truths while discovering a time when God unquestionably spoke to *you*.

After reading the whisper stories, we'll end with the third part in learning to hear the Lord's whispers: *explanation*. The final chapter ends our lesson by *explaining*—what the whispers are, to whom God will speak, and when, at one special time, He unquestionably did speak to His child.

⌒ꜩ   ⌒ꜩ   ⌒ꜩ

Through the following stories, your faith will be encouraged to hear His whispers—in your heart and through the Word. But what is faith? How much do we have, and how do we make it grow . . . ?

Two
Faith to Hear

Faith is what we hope for,
Not what we see.
Trusting in the Spirit,
Not the strength in me.

FAITH. WHAT EXACTLY IS IT? "NOW FAITH IS BEING SURE OF WHAT WE HOPE for and certain of what we do not see" (Hebrews 11:1 NIV).

Faith is the action of believing for what I'm hoping. It takes faith to believe beyond what we see, or expect to see in the future. Even a nonbeliever practices faith. Yet, if we place our faith in things other than God, we cannot please Him. We must first use our faith to believe that He exists because, ". . . without faith it is impossible to please God, because anyone who comes to him must believe that he exists and that he rewards those who earnestly seek him" (Hebrews 11:6 NIV).

Have you ever felt lacking in faith? There are times when I feel that lack, especially when I hear incredible stories of the fantastic faith exercised by others. These stories tend to leave me standing awestruck instead of motivated to be walking in faith daily. In fact, when I compare my faith to such great and wonderful acts of faith—I don't think I possess any faith at all. However, I'm reassured that the Word says we all possess a measure of faith and what the faith of a small seed can do: "if you have faith as a mustard seed, you will say to this mountain, 'Move from here to there,' and it will move; and nothing will be impossible for you" (Matthew 17:20b).

The mustard seed is very small, yet when it's planted in the soil and watered (though the seed itself dies), the plant that grows out of the seed is very large. This is a perfect example of how our faith grows. Like the seed, which dies in order for the plant to grow, our faith will grow when we die to relying merely on our own strength—choosing to trust fully in God's. Once, the Lord used a stubborn old generator to whisper into my heart—revealing whose strength I relied upon . . .

Faith in Our Strength—*Versus*—Faith in the Spirit

Since our family lives without electricity and we tap into a well for our water needs, we operate a generator near the well. The generator provides the electricity needed to pump water from the well to a holding tank. If the water in the tank runs dry, it calls for a trip to the generator to turn it on—refilling the tank.

On one particular day when I was home alone, the water tank ran dry. This meant a trip to the generator, a chore I'd usually rather leave to someone else . . . This generator isn't one of those fancy types that turn on by merely touching a button. I compare it to an old lawnmower I remember as a teen: a mechanical monster with a pull-rope that demanded I pull it with all my strength—only to be jerked back so fast I was certain it wanted to rip my arm off for dinner!

So there I stood over this cold monster, our generator. Reaching for the rope I pulled it with all my strength. It failed to turn on *and* fulfilled my greatest fears. Before I let go of the rope, it had yanked me back with such incredible force I felt like a cartoon character whose long, elastic arms stretched down to the ground like a chimpanzee's. We played tug-of-war for a while before I finally sat down and cried out to God, and I do mean *cried*. Getting up . . . wiping myself off, I stared down at the uncooperative *monster*, giving one last pull on the rope—and it started!

Yet, instead of jumping for joy and thanking God, as I should have, I was miffed. "OK, God," I asked. "Why do You wait until I'm upset and crying before You will answer me?" The Lord responded softly and whispered in my heart, "You didn't really want *My* help until you cried out. Why didn't you exercise your faith sooner?" Of course, the Lord was right. Striving to win the battle in my own strength, I hadn't sought God's help until I'd given up, completely frustrated that I couldn't do it on my own. The Lord began whispering to my heart, teaching me more about faith through this "whisper story."

Just as I'd rather have sent someone else to struggle with the generator, we often feel more comfortable sending someone else to have the faith needed for our problems. And in the same way I tried to fight the generator with my own muscle-power, many times we try to solve problems by exerting our own brute strength. But what power source do we rely on? "'Not by might nor by power, but by My Spirit,' Says the Lord of hosts" (Zechariah 4:6b).

We don't win our battles by our might or power, i.e., strength. We win our battles as our faith grows—by putting *less* trust in the weak arm of self and *more* in the strong hands of God. It's usually when we're knee-deep in our own weakness that we see most clearly how strong our God is . . .

"When I Am Weak, He Is Strong."

Two weeks before Christmas and the streets exploded with traffic. More than once I'd hit the brake pedal to keep from following a car too closely. A difficult decision I'd made earlier in the day preoccupied my mind and left me feeling weak in faith. Once again I allowed my vehicle to inch too closely to the car ahead of me. I stepped on the brake pedal again, but this time the car didn't respond. It kept speeding down its path! Desperately, I pumped the brake pedal; still no response.

The car won't stop. This can't be happening! I thought, beginning to panic.

My vehicle accelerated, rapidly approaching the car in front of me. Red lights started flashing on the long line of cars that stretched before me. Traffic was stopping! Empty cars lined the curbs on both sides of the narrow old road while holiday shoppers scurried about the sidewalks, searching for that special Christmas treasure. Every direction I frantically searched overflowed with people and cars. There was nowhere to go, nowhere to turn—and nowhere to stop.

How could I stop this automobile, which carried my precious children? Fast, serious prayers issued from my heart while forcing the brake pedal to the floorboard with all the strength and determination in my body. No response. The car continued racing toward the red lights just ahead of me. I needed to make a decision, and quick!

"Lord, what should I do?!" I prayed anxiously, but silently, not wanting to frighten the children.

Seeing an empty parking lot to my right, I quickly turned into it. Changing gears, I hoped to slow the car down. Second gear— no response. First gear—still no response. The car raced forward as though it intended to carry out a plan of its own. A solid brick wall towered to my right; a restaurant stood to my left, and a solid rock wall loomed straight ahead. I felt boxed in—with absolutely nowhere to go! Suddenly I spied a parking curb at the end of the lot, just in front of the rock wall. I headed for it. As the wheels hit the curb, I threw the shift lever into park, finally stopping the runaway car—just inches from the rock wall.

Sliding out of the driver's seat of the car, I caught a glimpse of my trembling hands—the only visible sign of the trauma we had just experienced.

My daughter Danielle said, "Mom, what are we doing *here*?"

I smiled. I had no idea why we'd parked in such a strange place, but I knew the Lord did. In that very same moment the Lord began to comfort me, and I heard the whispers of the Lord speak this Scripture into my heart, "My grace is sufficient for you, for My strength is made perfect in weakness" (2 Corinthians 12:9).

Losing control of the car had caused me to reflect on how weak I really was, and am daily. I realized I could trust God with my life when my brakes failed, *and* my difficult decisions in life. When we're strong or problem-free, it's easy to trust in our own strength, making decisions as we please. But it's in our weaknesses that we realize our need for God's intervention in our lives. When we're humble, we can admit how weak we are. God, however, is strong— we can trust Him with our whole life, rather than trusting in ourselves, or the solution we're expecting from God.

Faith isn't believing in God solving a problem using our solution, or even that God will solve our problem at all. True faith is believing in God alone. You see, God's solution to our problem is not always what our solution would be. I desired that the Lord solve my brake problem by miraculously repairing my brakes, rather than taking the course that left me weak and trembling. But the Lord knew exactly where my car would travel when He directed me to that parking lot. Every time I've looked in that parking lot since then, I've *never* seen it empty, as it was on the day my brakes failed.

My faith grew a little on that frightening day. I know God could have called me home to be with Him, but He didn't. But the fact that God spared my life isn't why my faith grew. Rather, I finally began to realize fully that I belong to God—that I am His, and He loves me—more than I could ever love myself. That's why I know I can trust Him . . . that we all can trust Him . . . because of His love for us.

Our faith needs to grow until we can trust God totally with our lives. Then we can pray as Jesus did on the night before His crucifixion, ". . . Father, all things *are* possible for You. Take this cup away from Me; nevertheless, not what I will, but what You *will*" (Mark 14:36).

When we trust God completely with our lives, we can stand in times of difficulty—just as these three Hebrew men did . . .

Three Hebrew Men

In the book of Daniel there is a story about three men who loved God. They were so faithful to Him that when King Nebuchadnezzar ordered them to bow down to his golden image or be thrown into the fiery furnace, they refused. This is what they told the king, who was threatening them with death:

> If that *is the case*, our God whom we serve is able to deliver us from the burning fiery furnace, and He will deliver *us* from your hand, O king. But if not, let it be known to you, O king, that we do not serve your gods, nor will we worship the gold image which you have set up. (Daniel 3:17, 18)

These men knew God could deliver them, yet they also knew God has His own will. They exercised their faith, but surrendered themselves to the will of God. This is how to pray as these men did: "Now this is the confidence that we have in Him, that if we ask anything according to His will, He hears us" (1 John 5:14).

Our faith will never override the will of God. On the other hand, we shouldn't just shrug our shoulders and say, "It must not be the will of God," because we're not exercising our believing faith. There are times when it's God's will that we wrestle to receive, as did faithful Jacob . . .

The Heart of Jacob

One Sunday when our Church served communion at the altar I reached into the basket to get a wafer and chose the smallest piece. I'm not at all sure why I did that, but I do know it gave me a small and silly pleasure in thinking I left larger pieces for someone else to take. Instantly I heard the whisper of the Lord and I didn't sense His pleasure with my actions.

The Lord whispered in my heart: "Do not choose the smaller portion of Me. My desire is that you have the heart of Jacob. Be eager and aggressive to receive from Me. If you take little—little you will receive."

Ouch! The Lord rebuked my actions, not because I chose a small wafer, but because the wafer represents Him. The Lord used my choice at the communion altar as an opportunity to reveal attitudes that kept me from receiving more from Him.

I began to think about what the Lord meant by having the "heart of Jacob" in the Old Testament. I knew that Jacob had wrestled with an angel of the Lord in order to get a blessing. I wondered if I would be willing to wrestle for a blessing, or whether I would just shrug my shoulders and say, "It must not be God's will." I often *want* to be aggressive as Jacob was, but I may lack the understanding to truly believe Jesus *wants* me to receive more from Him.

Why do I exercise such little faith when it comes to receiving from God? I wondered. Yet if I pursue anything in life, I want it to be the Lord—to be what He wants for me. Jesus taught that to enter the kingdom of heaven, we must come with the faith of a small child.

This faith is humble and sincere, but I also know *exactly* what a small child will do if he or she wants something—grab the biggest piece! And I *also* want more of Him . . . more of His touch in my life. Right there, I determined to show my changed attitude and prove that I am truly willing to wrestle for more of Him.

Communion time arrived again and Don, an elder in our Church, held the basket of wafers before me. Intent on finding the biggest piece, my focus kept me from noticing him watching me. I suddenly realized how silly I looked standing over the basket scouring its contents with my eyes, searching for the biggest cookie. Don greeted me . . . or at least it sounded like a greeting. Actually, I had no idea what he'd said. I had found the *biggest* piece!

I certainly felt humble taking the wafer back to my seat to take communion with my family. But I was rejoicing too! "Therefore whoever humbles himself as this little child is the greatest in the kingdom of heaven" (Matthew 18:4). I want the humble faith of a child—one who's willing to wrestle as Jacob did for the biggest blessing—never getting enough and always wanting more of Him!

My Prayer:

Lord, help me to see Your will more clearly so that I will know how to pray. Help me to increase my faith by trusting in You more, so that I can hear Your whispers, and move mountains through Your Spirit. Never let me be satisfied with a smaller portion, but help me to exercise faith to wrestle for more! Amen.

Through faith we hear the whispers of the Holy Spirit speaking truth to our hearts. But what is truth? How do we know it? How do we live in it once we know it . . .?

THREE
The Spirit Brings Truth

The Truth He reveals to you,
Is like a precious gem.
You never should compare yourself,
To anyone but Him.

WHAT IS TRUTH? HOW DO WE KNOW IT? HOW DO WE LIVE IN IT ONCE WE know it?

Relative Truth

Much of the world today views truth as relative. Relative truth is opinion based on circumstance, environment, and background. I learned a lot about relative truth from listening to a defense attorney in a college law class I attended. He based his speech on these two statements:

1. There is no such thing as right or wrong, moral or immoral, truth or lie, black or white—there is only gray.

This first statement is an opinion so, in itself, is a relative truth. To believe this statement is to believe there is no righteous God to whom we answer. The second statement is:

2. The majority vote of the people determines what is right, moral, or true.

This second statement is also a relative truth since the people's votes are based on opinion. Now think about that: Our opinions can't determine what is right, moral, or true! However, the majority vote of the people *does* reveal the condition of their hearts. What does the Bible say? We cannot rely on our hearts alone for what is right, moral, or true because, "The heart *is* deceitful above all *things*, And desperately wicked; Who can know it?" (Jeremiah 17:9).

When we base our country's laws or our own lives on an opinion of what we think is right, we are only fooling ourselves since, "There is a way *that seems* right to a man, But its end *is* the way of death" (Proverbs 14:12).

Instead of relying on our way or our opinion, we should seek to know God's truth revealed in the pages of the Word through the Holy Spirit. Worldly opinions can easily affect us when we don't seek truth here. Whatever opinions filter through society will filter across our pathway as well. And if we're not careful, they will enter our hearts. We are often unaware of how much these opinions affect us, and worse, they may sometimes *seem* right or true.

The Holy Spirit revealed something in my own life that taught me how deceiving my opinion could be. Although this opinion didn't lead to death, the Spirit used it to teach me a wonderful lesson on how to know truth, as well as the importance of living in it . . .

What's Your Opinion?

It's impossible to rush through a grocery store with a shopping cart for a few items with a cute baby on board. On this occasion, Jake was a magnet for every grandmother or baby-admirer who crossed our path. Just when I was making the final turn to dash for the checkout stand, a young woman with beautiful red hair stopped us. As she began comparing her baby to mine, much to my surprise I realized that she was talking to me as though I were a fellow redhead. It became difficult for me to focus on her conversation, since I kept trying to understand why she thought I had red hair. In fact, this baffled me so much, I completely forgot I was in a hurry!

A funny feeling came over me and I knew the Holy Spirit wanted to teach me something—something I didn't want to learn. Talking to the Lord on my way home I inquired, "Lord, I'm not a redhead, I'm a blonde. Why did she think my hair was red?" I could feel the soft whispers of the Holy Spirit gently questioning my desire to know the truth.

"What color is your hair? Are you sure?"

When my husband, Dan, came home I asked him for his opinion. "Dan, what color do you think my hair is?" Again to my surprise and annoyance, "*Red!*" he chirped, with the oversized grin of a leprechaun. My thoughts did not consist of how to thank my Irish husband for what he assumed would represent the *ultimate compliment*. Rather, I considered wiping the grin off his face—but settled for an unrestrained glare. After all, that was an insult to a "California Blonde!" (No pride here!) Have you ever noticed that the closer people come to our hearts the farther they move from our ears? I've decided that Dan and I are close, real close. (I actually *do* like red hair. The problem didn't begin with the color, but with my opinion of myself.)

Searching to find an opinion my ears *could* hear, I consulted my friend Lynn.

"Red!" Lynn insisted.

Still determined I was a blonde my opinion remained un-moved—but that still small voice spoke again. The Spirit asked me what I wrote on my driver's license for hair color. Blonde, of course! The very same hair color declared since I got my first driver's license at the age of sixteen. Again I could hear the soft whispers of the Holy Spirit, questioning my desire to know the truth. I must not have desired to know the truth very much, though, because I quickly forgot about these whispers . . . or at least I forgot until visiting, later, with my sister Irene.

Irene is a fantastic hairstylist, so I usually ask her to style my hair. This generally results in a game of "Let's Search for Donna's Gray Hairs." Once she finds a gray hair, it's pulled and announced with enormous satisfaction and delight. Then she'll take the colorless strand of hair in her fingers to examine it proudly as if she'd just won a prize. Next she'll push it in my face and exclaim, "Look, Donna, look how *white* it is!" I never thought I would say this but, sadly, the search for gray hairs didn't happen this time. Irene said bluntly, presuming I already knew, "Donna, your hair is getting *sooo* red!"

When your hairdresser says it, what else can you do? It still took time to adjust, but with some long looks in the mirror under bright lights, and with Irene's professional help, I finally accepted the truth. It was embarrassing to discover that there was some-thing in my life I hadn't seen truthfully. And worse, to know that I hadn't desired to know the truth, but strongly denied it while cling-ing to my own opinion.

How Can Worldly Opinions Affect Us?

After accepting the truth about my hair, I learned that our well water contains a large amount of iron. Shampooing daily in this water had gradually coated my hair with iron particles and changed it to a red color. The iron in my water is similar to the opinions in our world. Much the same way my hair changed color through the (unknown) influence of the iron in my water, the steady influence of worldly opinions can affect us. Just as I didn't realize that my hair had turned red, we may not realize it when we're thinking, acting, and living in ways that do not please God.

How could I look in the mirror day after day and not see the truth? Perhaps I saw only what I wanted to see. Truth is sometimes difficult to face. Even when we stare squarely at the facts we may choose to ignore them because we've grown so accustomed to our opinion that it is the only one that appears right and true. Growing up blonde as a child caused me to perceive myself as a blonde. I became so accustomed to being blonde that even when my hair experienced natural changes I retained my opinion. In order for me to know the truth about my actual hair color, I needed to compare or measure my opinion against a perfect source of truth. But what perfect source can we compare our opinions with to really see the truth?

What Source Do We Use to Know Truth?

The Holy Spirit began whispering to my heart again to teach me more about truth. In my mind, I could see a picture of myself standing among the native people of Africa with their jet-black hair. Then, in contrast, I saw another picture in my mind . . . but this time I stood among the native people of Sweden with their light blonde hair. The Africans considered me a blonde because they compared me to themselves. They saw a blonde. However, the fair-haired Swedes in my mental picture did not see a blonde. Since each group of people derived their opinions by comparing me against themselves and their own familiar circumstances, environment, and background, they could only arrive at a *relative* truth.

To know my true hair color, I couldn't compare my hair to other hair colors, or even ask the opinion of friends. To really know the truth, I found a hairdresser with a mirror and a good light. The hairdresser examined my hair with the light and, by looking intently into the mirror, revealed my true hair color.

How can we know the difference between truth and opinion? Between what does and doesn't please God? Can we measure ourselves by the opinions of this world? No. We should not compare ourselves to the best person we know. Comparing ourselves to others is similar to me comparing my hair color to other hair colors; it only supplied me with an opinion. To *really* know the truth about our lives, we need to listen to the whispers of the Holy Spirit through the Word and in our hearts. These whispers will always contain truth—as Jesus told us they would in this Scripture, "However, when He, the Spirit of truth, has come, He will guide you into all truth " (John 16:13a).

The Holy Spirit is much like the hairdresser in the story who shined a good light on the subject to see my true hair color in the mirror. The truth the Spirit shines into our hearts is the perfect resource by which to measure ourselves. His reality is not an opinion, which can change, but absolute truth, which doesn't. This perfect source is Jesus. He is the good "Light" that the Holy Spirit shines into our hearts. When the light of Jesus shines into our hearts, we can see clearly into the mirror, the Word. Then the mirror will reveal truth to us. If we measure ourselves by anything else, we gain only a false perception of ourselves, and we won't recognize worldly opinions that do not please God. But once we really recognize and accept the truth, revealed by the Word, we can then make the wise choice to live by it.

Living by the Truth

Hearing and recognizing truth does not mean we're living by the truth. The Lord desires that we become "doers" of the Word and not "hearers only." What is the difference between the two?

> But be doers of the word, and not hearers only, deceiving your-selves. For if anyone is a hearer of the word and not a doer, he is like a man observing his natural face in a mirror; for he observes himself, goes away, and immediately forgets what kind of man he was. But he who looks into the perfect law of liberty and continues *in it*, and is not a forgetful hearer but a doer of the work, this one will be blessed in what he does. (James 1:22–25)

I've read this Scripture many times, but now when I read it I feel foolish. I feel just like the man who looked into the scriptural mirror, but kept on living by opinions rather than changing his behavior to live a life that was a true reflection of truth that the mirror revealed. The image we see in a physical mirror reflects our outward appearance. Beauty is all around us; life would not be so pleasing without it. Yet, it's foolish to elevate and admire beauty alone because someday it will fade. The Word is our spiritual mirror. It reveals our inward appearance. But what area is God interested in? "For *the Lord does* not *see* as man sees; for man looks at the outward appearance, but the Lord looks at the heart" (1 Samuel 16:7b).

We need to cultivate that inner beauty which will please God and last an eternity. Inner beauty grows when we love truth and seek it out for our lives. Only by insisting upon the truth can we live by the truth and strive to change what displeases God—becoming real doers of His holy Word.

My Prayer:

Lord, we live in a confusing world where truth is hard to know. Help me to know Your truth in every area of my life. Expose any of my opinions that are not pleasing to You—in my heart, in my relationships, and in all of my life. Help me to live in Your truth . . . that I may live a godly life pleasing to You. Amen.

☙   ☙   ☙

If we grieve the Holy Spirit by rejecting the truth He brings, He will become silent and we won't hear His whispers. What other factors can hinder us from hearing? And what can we do to make certain we will hear clearly when He does speak . . . ?

Four
When You Cannot Hear

You've given over all your thoughts,
Now you meditate on Him.
You're clean and pure—you're shining
Your light before all men.

HOW CAN WE KEEP OUR THOUGHTS PURE? WHAT HAPPENS WHEN WE DON'T control our thoughts?

Pollution

Feeding baby Jake his milk was turning into a difficult chore. He would drink for only a few seconds before crying out in frustration. I started getting frustrated, too, until I realized something very simple was keeping him from getting his milk: a stuffed up nose prevented him from drinking and breathing at the same time. This called for a motherly chore I thoroughly dislike—cleaning out a baby's nose. It was an unpleasant experience for both of us, and he screamed loudly to make sure I knew it. Jake didn't understand why I would do such a thing to him, but his appetite prevailed and he began drinking happily again—forgetting all about his nose cleaning. The Lord whispered in my heart teaching me that we sometimes bear resemblance to my son. As it had Jake's nose, pollution can clog our minds. Jesus tells us clearly where these pollutions come from:

> It is the thought-life that pollutes. For from within, out of men's hearts, come evil thoughts of lust, theft, murder, adultery, wanting what belongs to others, wickedness, deceit, lewdness, envy, slander, pride and all other folly. All these vile things come from within; they are what pollute you and make you unfit for God. (Mark 7:20b–23 TLB)

All such thoughts as these are sin. They pollute our minds and prevent us from receiving our "spiritual milk"—the spiritual teaching we're given and our hearing of the whispers of God. When we allow sinful thoughts to have a place in our minds, we won't be able to hear the whispers of God. Instead, we must do as this Scripture instructs us, "Turn at my rebuke; Surely I will pour out my spirit on you; I will make my words known to you" (Proverbs 1:23).

When we repent and turn away from sin we will hear the whispers of God. Then we need to keep the pollution out.

Keeping Pollution Out

Have you ever caught yourself reading a book or listening to someone, then realized your thoughts have drifted somewhere else? Our minds are naturally unruly and sometimes difficult to control because they are always busy. However, the problem isn't *how* busy our minds are, rather *what* our minds are busy with. It's easy to say, "Have pure thoughts," yet this can be difficult to do. We *can* do it if we obey this Scripture, "take captive every thought to make it obedient to Christ" (2 Corinthians 10:5b NIV).

This means that when we realize our thoughts do not please God, we take active control of our minds—rejecting impure thoughts as soon as they try to enter. Then, to keep our minds free of unwanted thoughts, we replace them with prayer, reading of the Word, listening to uplifting worship music, or enjoying other believers. Strangely, the Lord used a sewing machine to show me what happens when we fill our minds with sinful pollutions . . .

Oodles of Noodles

While taking my sewing machine out of storage, I discovered that egg noodles filled every hollow space in it. It seems mice had discovered my rarely used machine, and had stored their food reserves there for the entire winter. I shook the heavy machine briskly to loosen the noodles—but only a few fell to the floor. I knew that if I ever wanted to use this machine again I faced the tedious task of removing the troublesome noodles.

For the next several hours I pulled out noodles, but could only reach two or three at time. I removed hundreds of those nasty egg noodles, which crammed every nook and cranny of my machine, and just when I thought the job was completed, I found more! It felt to me like that machine was somehow holding on to every noodle as if it were trying to prevent me from removing them! But after removing the last noodle, I stood over the freed machine—exhausted but proud. At that very moment I heard the soft whispers of the Lord speaking to my heart. In my mind I saw a picture of the sewing machine. Then I saw the bottom plate removed and, all at once, hundreds of egg noodles falling out. At last I understood! If I had removed the bottom plate of the machine I could have cleaned it all out in seconds, *versus* the hours of exasperating work I'd doggedly done. I lost the proud look rather quickly and began to hear a whispered teaching from the Holy Spirit.

He compared those noodles that kept my machine from working properly to sinful thoughts that hinder us as believers. The same way the mice filled the machine with one noodle at a time, we can slowly fill our minds with thoughts that don't please God. These thoughts may continue unnoticed because they filter in . . . just one thought at a time. By not rejecting them, we may begin reacting to people or circumstances with the kind of unproductive attitudes that can fill us with bitterness, anger, and unforgiveness. When this happens, we cannot hear the voice of God or function the way He desires for us, doing His will. But there is hope. Because God desires fellowship with us, He will remove anything that prevents it—assuming we *allow* Him to do so.

Similar to my machine-cleaning, this sin "removal" process becomes a slow and tedious job if we hold on to the pollutants. These are the things that prevent us from hearing the whispers of God and keep us from doing His good works. But, by being obedient to God's promptings and doing His will, the cleansing process becomes much easier. Once cleared of pollutants, we will function properly, just as my machine did. Then we will hear the whispers of the Holy Spirit in our hearts.

What if after going through this cleaning process we feel confident that our hearts no longer contain pollutants, but we still aren't hearing the whispers? If our thoughts are focusing in the wrong area, it can prevent us from having the peace of God and from hearing His whispers . . .

Peace of God

One Sunday during Church worship time I felt the whispers of the Lord speaking to my heart. First He told me that the hearts of many believers are heavy. Some Christians know this heaviness well. Others remain unaware of it because, from carrying it so long, the weight seems a natural part of their lives.

Next the Lord gave me a very small insight into the heavenly kingdom. I felt an overwhelming peace and love. At this moment the Lord whispered a question into my heart, "If you remain with Me would you worry about your children or the affairs of your life?"

"No, Lord, only You truly matter. When I am in Your presence, I know You will tend to my children, and my concerns of this world just don't seem to matter anymore." Then the Lord spoke softly in my heart, "Your job is not done on earth, so you must remain for now. Do you still trust your children and affairs to Me?" I realized then that I carried a heavy heart too. So in my own heart I responded, "Yes, Lord, but help me to keep my eyes and mind on You." The Lord explained that many of His people bear heavy hearts because their eyes and minds keep focusing on the things of this earth. Where should we focus . . . ?

Focusing and Finding Peace

Walking through our property I often focus my eyes on the pathway at my feet. The Lord drew my attention to this while I walked, and in a gentle whisper in my heart asked me why I didn't lift my head to see all the beauty. I couldn't think of a good reason. Maybe it's a bad habit; maybe I'm afraid of stubbing my toe; or maybe it's because I'm so short and always looking up that it's a strain to lift my head! Then the Lord reminded me of a time when my shortsightedness almost caused an accident . . .

My high school offered professional driver's training. On the day we were to drive in *real* cars, the teacher divided the class into groups of four. Somehow I was elected to drive first, so the instructor unceremoniously placed the keys in my hand, turned and walked around to the passenger's side, entered, and sat down. My three friends started giggling and joking and got on board in the back seat. With keys in hand, I took a long look at the driver's seat and sank slowly into it. The instructor received fair warning on how the next hour would go when I gave a sheepish smile, lifted up the key and asked, "Where does this go?" My audience in the back seat laughed, but I'm not sure if they fully understood my seriousness.

Maneuvering out the driveway to leave the school curb, my eyes focused on the pavement just in front of the hood of the car. To my right the edge of a thirty-foot cliff dropped down to a football field. With my focus being so shortsighted, I couldn't see that we were heading straight for the ledge. The car quickly traveled farther than the spot where my eyes were focusing. My instructor braked for me and very wisely told me to look ahead so I could see where I was going. Of course, the three in the back seat burst out in laughter but, more embarrassing to me, it wouldn't be the last time!

Once we reached the main street, I focused on the road about ten feet in front of the hood. This felt safe to me, but when we reached a curve in the road the car came upon it too fast to see it and react in time. Again the instructor rescued me, and again back-seat laughter filled the vehicle. This time the instructor showed me exactly where to focus. If I kept my eyes focused where the instructor told me to, I found I responded in plenty of time in anticipating curves in the road ahead. I loved it. From then on, I had no more trouble. My classmates were a little disappointed that I figured things out, since they had taken great pleasure in my training trials. I, on the other hand, enjoyed the peace and quiet! This is similar to the peace that the Lord wants us to enter. Here's why:

The Lord is our instructor. He wants us to learn where to focus so that we'll live in His peace. When we learn where to focus, it's a matter of perspective, not blindness. We limit our perspective when we look too closely at a situation, just as I did with the car. But when I looked up and out beyond the hood of the car I could see both in the distance and up close. I didn't limit my view—I expanded it. It's the same when we focus on the kingdom. We don't lose sight of what happens around us when we look up and out—our perspective improves! If our minds focus only on the things of this earth (our troubles and cares), we will carry heavy hearts as I did. But if we focus on the Lord's kingdom we can live in His peace and hear His voice.

When I'm driving now, it's an automatic response to focus up and out. However, I still struggle to keep my eyes focused up and out when I'm walking. It's the same with our spiritual lives here on earth. We live in peace in the conquered areas where we've learned to focus and trust in God. But we may struggle in other areas where we have to work harder at entering a trusting peace. Here we see God's response to our shortsightedness, "But You, O Lord, *are* a shield for me, My glory and the One who lifts up of my head" (Psalm 3:3).

The Lord desires that we enter His peace, and when He sees our shortsightedness He lifts up our heads and reminds us where to focus! The Lord reminded my friend, Dora, where her focus should be and where it shouldn't be. Here is her story of the Lord's whispers to her:

❦ ❦ ❦

One day I was sitting in the office doing my work when the Lord asked me, "Dora, where do you look when you are driving your car?"

"What?" I asked, quite puzzled by this sudden question that came out of nowhere.

"Where do you look when you are driving your car?" He repeated His question.

"Well straight ahead, of course," I answered, thinking this was a very strange question.

"Why is it that you use your rearview mirror?" He pressed on.

"To look at the cars behind me . . . to see how close they are, and to be aware of what may occur. Basically, for guidance," I responded, very pleased with my answer, but still quite puzzled at this inquiry.

Then the Lord said, "Dora, you have been looking in the rearview mirror as you have been living life for quite a while now. You do not drive your car by focusing your eyes in the rearview mirror. You look straight ahead because you want to see where you are going. That is as it should be as you live your life.—Forget the things of the past and do not dwell on them. Just as you drive your car, you may give those things of the past a glance or two but you must continue on to the things I have before you."

"Oh," I responded, with a heavy sigh. "I didn't realize I was living in the past, looking back at what could have been, and thinking how much better it would be now if only I would have done things differently." I suppose there was an element of regretfulness. I was encouraged that the Lord cared enough to speak a word of correction to me. It is a secure feeling to know that when I get off track He puts me back on the path He has set before me. I'm reminded of what the Apostle Paul, so long ago, said to the church at Philippi:

> Brethren, I do not count myself to have apprehended; but one thing *I do*, forgetting those things which are behind and reaching forward to those things which are ahead, I press toward the goal for the prize of the upward call of God in Christ Jesus. (Philippians 3:13, 14)

Giving this corrective word some thought, I began to see that I not only set my sights on the rearview mirror, but also on the sideview mirrors. We use these mirrors for guidance, but we don't focus on them. I realized I focused on others on this upward walk and compared myself to them. I saw the deeds of

others and how much better they were doing, instead of focusing on what the Lord wanted to do through me.

⟡   ⟡   ⟡

Thank you, Dora. If we live in faith, focusing on the kingdom of
God instead of our feet in fear of stumbling, our past in regretfulness, or our sideviews in pride or envy of others, this Scripture makes
us a sure promise, "You will keep *him* in perfect peace, *Whose* mind
is stayed *on You*, Because he trusts in You" (Isaiah 26:3).

I want this kind of peace in my life! No matter what curves of
life lie ahead on our pathway, we can enjoy perfect peace. This
doesn't mean we won't feel the curves as we hit some of them but
that, if we keep our minds focused on the heavenly realm our perspective will improve and we will experience His peace. By focusing on Christ and the heavenly realm, however, we shouldn't
become so "religious" that we become totally useless here on earth.
Rather, as we deepen our relationship with Christ, He will lift our
minds to think pure thoughts so we can hear His whispers.

My Prayer:

Lord, show me when my thoughts contain pollutants that do not
please You. Cleanse me of the sins that prevent me from hearing
Your voice and doing Your good works. Then help me to focus on
Your kingdom, so my perspective is broadened and not merely
focused on my own concerns. Lead me in Your peace—the peace
described in Psalms 23:

> THE Lord *is* my shepherd; I shall not want.
> He makes me to lie down in green pastures;
> He leads me beside the still waters. He restores my soul;
> He leads me in the paths of righteousness
> For His name's sake.

Yea, though I walk through the valley of the shadow of death,
I will fear no evil;
For You *are* with me; Your rod and Your staff, they comfort me.
You prepare a table before me in the presence of my enemies;
You anoint my head with oil; My cup runs over.
Surely goodness and mercy shall follow me
All the days of my life;
And I will dwell in the house of the Lord Forever.
(Psalm 23) Amen.

☙   ☙   ☙

The words we speak reveal our attitudes of the heart . . . so we need to judge our words to see if they please God. Do our words bring a sting of death and destruction, or are they as sweet as honey—giving life to the hearer . . . ?

FIVE
When Words
Have to Be Eaten

Your words are sweet as honey.
They're wise, sure, and true.
Your words are not so many,
But a carefully chosen few.

WORDS CAN HURT OR SOOTHE THE SOUL. HOW CAN WE TEST THEM TO SEE IF they're ugly words that bring death and destruction or good, fruitful words that give life?

Choosing Carefully

Sitting on the porch one day—soaking in the sun and thinking of nothing in particular—I noticed a bee squirming in a puddle of water. I must admit I lacked compassion for him, since bees had stung my daughter Catherine twice in the last few days.

All of a sudden from under the porch a tiny frog, not much bigger than the bee, leaped upon the drowning insect. Mouth open wide, he snapped up the bee for a quick easy dinner. You can just imagine what that angry bee did—and how quickly the frog spit him out! The wounded frog leaped away as fast as he could. I have no doubt the frog learned that if he doesn't want another stinger he'd better learn wisdom when choosing his next meal.

Just when the frog spewed the bee out of its mouth the Lord whispered into my heart this teaching: We need to learn wisdom when choosing our words because, similar to the bee, in time they may harm us because: "Your souls aren't harmed by what you eat, but by what you think and say!" (Mark 7:15, 16 TLB). Just as the sting of a bee, our words are so powerful they too can sting, as this Scripture describes: "Death and life *are* in the power of the tongue, And those who love it will eat its fruit" (Proverbs 18:21).

Harmful words will sting not only others, but our own souls as well. Our words can minister death and destruction, but they can also give the sweetness of life. Maybe if the frog had waited and followed the bee home, he could have exchanged the stinger for a mouth full of honey, since "Pleasant words *are like* a honeycomb, Sweetness to the soul and health to the bones" (Proverbs 16:24). Well, maybe not . . . but if we could get wisdom when choosing our words, we would become much slower to speak. Ahh, but like that frog we all have difficulty waiting for the right moment to speak, and also in controlling our tongues.

The Lord gave me these Scriptures to illustrate two opposite ways of speaking. These Scriptures show us the life-giving words *versus* those words that inflict the sting of death:

Life—*Versus*—Death

1. Blessing	vs.	Cursing	James 3:8–10
2. Encouraging	vs.	Nagging	Ephesians 4:29 / Prov. 27:15
3. Humility	vs.	Prideful boasting	James 4:6, 16
4. Not swearing	vs.	Swearing	James 5:12 / Lev. 19:12
5. Contentment	vs.	Complaining	Heb. 13:5 / Phil. 2:14
6. Soft words	vs.	Harsh words	Prov. 15:1

7. Keeping trusts	vs.	Gossiping	Prov. 17:9
8. Wisdom	vs.	Foolish jesting	Eccles. 9:17 / Prov. 26:18, 19
9. Truthful	vs.	Lying	Prov. 12:22
10. Mercy	vs.	Judging	1 Pet.4:8 / Matt. 7:1
11. Few words	vs.	Many words	Prov. 10:19
12. Confesses sin	vs.	Conceals sin	Prov.28:13
13. Rebuking the wise	vs.	Rebuking the foolish	Prov. 9:7–9
14. Weeping with those who weep	vs.	Singing to the heavyhearted	Rom. 12:15 / Prov. 25:20
15. Seeking solutions by praying	vs.	Positive confession techniques	Phil. 4:6,7 / Matt. 5:36

The Lord whispered to me a further explanation of items number 14 and 15, above:

Weeping With Those Who Weep—*Versus*—

Singing to the Heavyhearted

This Scripture explains the cold heart of someone who sings to a heavy heart, "*Like* one who takes away a garment in cold weather, *And like* vinegar on soda, *Is* one who sings songs to a heavy heart" (Proverbs 25:20).

Taking a coat away from someone when they're cold is a cruel thing to do. Also, vinegar causes a reaction when poured on soda. So, when we sing to the heavyhearted it's so cruel it causes a reaction—and not a good one! In the book of Job we find a good example of singing to a heavy heart.

Satan had attacked Job, destroying his children, his health, wealth—everything but his wife and his life. When his friends came to visit, what do you suppose they did? They quoted the Scripture, accused and judged him. What were they doing? Singing to a heavyhearted Job. They didn't try to help Job. They wanted to rub Job's nose in his troubles, as if to say, "We knew you weren't righteous Job, and we feel better now that we can look down our noses at you!"

Another way we can sing to the heavyhearted is to literally try to cheer up someone who is enduring turmoil, trials, or grief. What a friend wants and needs from us is the same thing we want from them: comfort and love. We can offer such great compassion for others that we can actually feel the heart of our neighbors. Then we will truly weep when they weep. Such an act is not to be confused with pity; rather, it's an expression of true love. This Scripture tells us exactly how God wants us to respond to people in good times and in bad: "Rejoice with those who rejoice, and weep with those who weep" (Romans 12:15).

When we see someone hurting we fulfill this Scripture by being careful not to accuse, judge, or quote Scripture too quickly. Rather, we should show the love of Christ by offering compassion, then don't forget to rejoice when they rejoice! We can rejoice together when we seek solutions first through prayer . . .

**Seeking Solutions by Praying—*Versus*—
Seeking Solutions by Positive Confession**

While cleaning out the refrigerator, I found a small pottery bowl full of leftover gravy. Since Danielle was playing close by, I asked her to empty it out onto our compost pile. Her sweet, blue eyes lit up since she knew this was a "big kid" chore. When she stepped outside with the clay bowl, the remembrance of another recently broken fruit bowl came to my mind. I ran to the window to watch her. But instead of dread over what might happen to my bowl, I found myself excited to see her delight in the task and the carefulness she exercised as she removed the skin of solid fat from the bowl. At that moment the Lord whispered into my heart.

"Just as you delight in your child, I delight over My children when they remove the fat from their vessels." Then the Spirit began teaching me what this meant. The Word refers to us as a clay vessel or a kind of bowl, and in the Old Testament we see that God considered fat the choicest part of the sacrifice. God told the priests to reserve it for Him. The priests could not take a portion of it. The priest Eli had two sons who committed many sins, and one was taking and eating this fat. Eli's sons soon came to a bad ending. When they ate the fat set aside and reserved only for God, they were actually showing by their actions *who* the god of their lives was—themselves.

The fat in the vessel is a symbol of anyone who sets himself up as his own god. This happens when there is rebellion toward God in the heart. The clay vessel full of fat symbolizes a Christian full of rebelliousness toward God. In this state, we will seek within ourselves to find solutions to the problems of life instead of trusting God and seeking His solutions in prayer.

One way we may be seeking our own solution is through "positive confession" or "claiming" techniques. These unbiblical techniques teach people how to control their circumstances by making a claim based on a Scripture, and insisting that God must respond. The Scripture may be a true promise, or it may be a false interpretation of one. Either way, our demanding approach shows clearly where faith is being placed—in self.

Naturally, we *do* rely on God to fulfill His promises. This is not to say that we should allow Satan to rob us of the blessings or promises of God. But if we quote scriptural promises, it is to remind and encourage, or to fight the enemy. We trust in God, not self, to fulfill His promises because our human words didn't speak the universe into existence—God's did. This Scripture shows how much power we possess in and of ourselves: "Nor shall you swear by your head, because you cannot make one hair white or black" (Matthew 5:36).

No matter how positive our spoken claims, we cannot change even one hair on our own heads. Our mighty God is much greater than a genie in an old lamp, waiting for our commands. Our next Scripture paints a beautiful picture, which reveals our true relationship with God, "Know that the Lord, He *is* God; *It is* He *who* has made us, and not we ourselves; *We are* His people and the sheep of His pasture" (Psalms 100:3).

Instead of using positive confession, or claiming techniques to solve life's problems, we seek God's solutions through prayer. How do we make our requests known to God? This next Scripture tells us, "Be anxious for nothing, but in everything by prayer and supplication, with thanksgiving, let your requests be made known to God" (Philippians 4:6).

Through prayer we see results from God, not through claiming techniques that demand our own solutions. Demanding only reveals that our faith is not in God, but in self. We cannot serve both self and God. Positive claiming doesn't give life, but ultimately brings the sting of death because it serves self. Prayer is life-giving because our faith is in God, and so it serves God. How can we tell the difference between these words spoken in the self-serving interests of the world and words spoken purely in the interests of God?

Words from God, or from the World?

How can we know what is of God and what isn't? We cannot trust the best person we know to always offer us truth. In the book of Matthew, Jesus warned the disciples of His coming death and resurrection. Peter didn't want to believe this was God's will, so he rebuked Christ. Then Jesus turned to Peter and said, "Get behind Me, Satan! You are a stumbling block to Me; for you are not setting your mind on God's interest, but man's" (Matthew 16:23b NASB).

Jesus did not actually mean that Peter was Satan, but that the intent of the words Peter said came from Satan, and not from God. But how can we tell the difference between words said in the world's interest and words spoken in God's interest? Easy. We can recognize the difference as easily as separating apples from oranges . . .

Telling Apples from Oranges

I remember a time in my life when several Christians wounded me. Their wounding words were spoken from the interests of the world and not from the interest of God. But why didn't I recognize their source then and spare myself the sorrow? During the time I still hurt from these remarks, the Lord whispered to me by showing me through some orange juice what I had done wrong.

Opening the freezer door, I took out a can of orange juice. Taking the lid off I noticed it looked unusual, so I poured the contents into a pitcher to get a better view of the frozen pulp. It still didn't look right. I decided that water might make a difference in its appearance, so I began filling the empty can with water and stirring it into the concentrated juice. Stirring didn't make it look more like orange juice either, so I smelled it. Hmmm . . . Something didn't seem right. Reaching into the trash I grabbed the empty juice can I had just tossed out and read the label. In big bold letters across the can it read "Orange Juice."

"Well, that settles it," I said. "It has to be orange juice." Giving it one last stir I tasted the juice from the spoon as I pulled it out of the pitcher. "This doesn't taste like orange juice!" I said, puzzled again. The taste was too weak to determine what was wrong, so I poured the juice into a tall glass and took a drink. "This isn't orange juice—it's *apple juice!*" I said with absolute certainty. Just then, I heard the whispers of the Lord teaching me.

"This is what you did with the words that were spoken to you. If you'd tested the fruit before you swallowed, you could have rejected the bad fruit and spared yourself much sorrow."

When wounded in the past by words of men or women who had their own interests in mind rather than God's, I just ate the fruit given to me. I didn't stop to question, or pray. After all, these were fellow believers who wore the familiar label, "Christian." *The label doesn't always guarantee the type of fruit offered!* Just as I had discovered apple juice even though the label was marked "Orange Juice." If I had first tested the words to identify where the fruit originated, I would have recognized its source: worldliness. Here is a list of the nine spiritual fruits, which you can use to test what words are offered to you, "But the fruit of the Spirit is love, joy, peace, patience, kindness, goodness, faithfulness, gentleness and self-control. Against such things there is no law" (Galatians 5:22,23 NIV). We use this list of fruits to test the words people offer us, but we also use it to test our own words as well. May all our speaking bring glory to God and not self.

My Prayer:

Lord, "Let the words of my mouth and the meditation of my heart Be acceptable in Your sight, O Lord, my strength and my Redeemer" (Psalm 19:14). Amen.

Our words can be life-giving as we learn to love with Christ's love. What's flawed with our love, and how can we begin to love with Christ's love? What does "unconditional love" mean, and how do we "turn the other cheek" as He did, in love . . . ?

SIX

His Tender Love

Be wise as a serpent,
Gentle as a dove,
A good example
Of Jesus' love.

HOW CAN WE LOVE WITH CHRIST'S LOVE?

Love's Passion

The word "love" refers to a variety of feelings, which can range from our love for chocolate, love for our cats and dogs, love for our sweetheart, and even our love for God. The passion of our love, which varies from one object of affection to another, is a good thing. However, the "temperamental" kind of love, which fluctuates according to our moods, isn't. The Lord showed me through some loaves of bread just how temperamental our love is . . .

Yeasted Loaves

Before I discovered that wonderful kitchen appliance called the "bread maker," I labored at producing bread by hand. Bread baking days were a real treat for the family. If I baked on cold days, it warmed the kitchen and filled the house with a delicious aroma.

On this occasion, the snow outside made it the perfect day for baking bread. I followed all of the procedures as before, but something was wrong. When I took the loaves out of the oven, instead of big, fluffy loaves I found flat loaves that had turned out hard, dry, and tasteless. Disappointed? To say the least! My vision of enjoying a steaming soft piece of bread smothered in butter was now ruined! I could sense a teaching coming. Honestly, I admit I didn't say, "Yes Lord, whisper in my heart and teach me." Rather, I'm somewhat embarrassed to say that I responded with a pout and said, "You mean my bread's ruined because You want to teach me something?" I'm so glad that the Lord is good; He taught me the lesson anyway.

"Temperamental"

The Lord whispered in my heart—telling me that the yeast within this hard, dry, and tasteless bread is like our natural love. Many times the Word refers to yeast as a symbol of sin. This doesn't mean that anything is wrong with yeast; it's merely a symbol.

Yeast is the main ingredient in bread that makes it rise to be soft, moist, and delicious. In spite of that, the most frequent reason for failure in breadmaking is because of the temperamental behavior of yeast. Yeast is very sensitive to its environment, requiring just the right temperature and care. If the water yeast is dissolved in is too cold, it won't be activated and the bread won't rise. If the water is too hot, the yeast becomes spoiled and, again it won't rise. In both cases the bread will be hard, dry, and tasteless.

Human love, with its sinful nature, is just as temperamental as the yeast. When we become hurt, disappointed, or rejected, and our expectations in life have grown cold, our love doesn't flourish. On the other hand if life gives us only abundance of pleasure, or if we hotly pursue only selfish desires, our love is also spoiled. Often we respond by growing hard, indifferent, and bitter. The Lord was right, this temperamental yeast does remind me of our love. Just as yeast is the main ingredient to make soft, moist, and delicious bread, love is the main ingredient to make life easy, pleasurable, and exciting. I'm grateful for the natural emotion of love. But human love, with its sinful nature, is just too *temperamental* to express the love of Christ to a hurting world—Jesus shows us a better way. He said, "If anyone desires to come after Me, let him deny himself, and take up his Cross daily, and follow Me" (Luke 9:23b).

Denying ourselves and taking up our Cross daily means that we die to our sinful nature, with our natural responses. This is not a daily physical death: that is impossible. Nor is it a ritual we perform daily to remind us of Christ's death. No, this death of our self-will is an attitude of the heart—one we would do well to remember daily, moment by moment, to serve Christ and live for Him rather than self. It is only by taking up our Cross daily and dying to self that we become capable of loving with Christ's love. A good example of dying to self and our temperamental (natural) responses to others is found in what Jesus said in this Scripture: "But I tell you, Do not resist an evil person. If someone strikes you on the right cheek, turn to him the other also" (Matthew 5:39 NIV).

Is this one of your favorite verses in the Bible? I didn't underline it in *my* Bible, or at least not until the Lord revealed its meaning and how to apply it to my life. I thought this Scripture meant that when someone hit me I needed to passively respond by allowing him or her to hit me again. In fact, encouraging the person to strike again! It was a relief to discover this is not the correct meaning of this Scripture. The Lord used this next Scripture to help me understand what it means to turn the other cheek: "Behold, I am sending you out like sheep in the midst of wolves; be wary *and* wise as serpents, and be innocent (harmless, guileless, and without falsity) as doves" (Matthew 10:16 AMP).

Wolves kill sheep–and remember we're the sheep! This sounds worse than someone striking us on the cheek! Jesus used the serpent (snake) and dove to give us a picture of how He wants us to respond to these wolves—the ones who want to kill us, as well as the ones who strike us. He said to, ". . . be wise as serpents, and gentle as doves." We are to imitate the snake that is wary and wise and the dove that is innocent, harmless, guileless and without falsity. Relating to the dove appeared rather easy; on the contrary, relating to a snake seemed impossible—until the day an uninvited snake slithered into my home . . .

The Snake

I didn't want to share the house with this black and yellow racer, and since no one could come to my rescue, the removal job became mine. This particular racer appeared to possess wisdom. He obviously preoccupied himself in looking for a way to escape from what he thought created a dangerous situation—me. He never moved in my direction, but always kept a safe distance. It didn't matter how careful I was; he anticipated my every move. When he wanted a new hiding place, he remained very still. He watched and waited patiently to make sure the situation was safe. Then he ducked quickly into his carefully selected hiding place and stayed there until I disturbed him once more. Boy, was I thankful when Kevin came home to rescue me. My son put on a pair of gloves and headed for the snake. Within minutes, Kevin held the racer in his hands and placed the snake safely outside the house. Kevin was very glad he'd put the gloves on, because the snake had tried repeatedly to strike him during this maneuver.

The Holy Spirit whispered in my heart, teaching me about this snake. Just as the racer carefully made his decisions about where and when to move next, so do we need to be careful to detect dangerous situations and respond to them wisely. This is what the Scripture means when it says we are to imitate the snake—behaving wisely and warily. But how do we respond if we become cornered with no way of escape? The Lord showed me just how to respond through a dove. I *thought* I related more to a dove than to a snake, but after Dan brought two doves home, I changed my mind . . .

The Dove

I had gone to the store for a few items. When I returned, I discovered that Dan had come home early from work. The kids all ran to greet me, "Daddy brought home some birds!" They led the way, hopping and dancing, to the garage to show me their new pets. Once inside, we all stood over the box that held the birds. There two beautiful gray doves huddled together while the Fitzpatrick family squirmed at the possibility of touching—or maybe even getting to hold—one of these gentle creatures. Dan lifted one of the doves up out of the box, and I couldn't resist. I reached out, touching the soft feathers on his head, and spoke to him. When Dan opened his hands the bird became frightened and flew up into the rafters of the garage to try and escape. Kevin came to the rescue again, but this time he didn't need gloves. He climbed up to the rafters and brought the bird down without any struggle. I watched in awe at the gentle response of this dove. Even when Kevin cornered him, he didn't even flutter; he just went along gently and sweetly. In my mind, I saw the sharp difference between the snake's response and the dove's response to being cornered. I knew exactly which one was most like me. Just then, the Lord whispered into my heart, showing me how I need to imitate the snake in one way and the dove in another.

Wary and Wise as a Snake / Gentle as a Dove

The snake exhibited wisdom by being wary and wise in surveying the situation. This is how we should imitate the snake. It is wisdom to identify a bad situation before it happens and to look for a way to remove ourselves if need be. But we don't want to respond as the snake did when it was cornered. The snake's first response was to duck, and if I hadn't bothered the snake it would have remained in a ducking position. When ducking didn't work and the snake became cornered once more it began striking. These responses of the snake are comparable to the natural responses we must seek to change or "die to." If there is no way of escaping danger and we become cornered, instead of responding like the snake, we can *choose* to imitate the trusting response of the dove.

The dove also tried to escape from what it thought was dangerous but, when cornered, the dove responded with gentleness. So we see the contrast of being wary and wise as the snake, but responding as a dove: that is, innocent, harmless, guileless, and without falsity. If someone strikes us physically, mentally, or emotionally, like the snake, our usual and natural response is either to duck or to strike back. Instead of reacting in fear that ducks, or anger that strikes back, our reaction can be as wise as the snake's, yet loving as the dove's. If we *die to* our natural responses we can respond with God's love.

Suddenly the Holy Spirit reminded me of a time when several people struck me emotionally. I responded by ducking from these people—trying to prevent any further damage. Out of fear, I'd remained in a perpetual "ducking position." In this position I felt safe, but it prevented me from giving and receiving God's love.

This is a hard habit to break. Getting struck had caused me to have an overly cautious response to everyone. When the Lord revealed my actions to me, I recognized attitudes and responses within myself that were neither wise nor loving. It's an ongoing (daily) process of dying to self that prefers to respond as the snake by ducking in fear, which leads to alienation, or striking back in anger, which leads to bitterness.

The Lord always lets us choose how we'll respond to our world. If we respond to others by ducking or by striking back, we cannot give or receive the Lord's love. But He doesn't want us to respond with this kind of temperamental love. Rather, with His love that is both wise *and* loving. However, to "turn the other cheek" we don't intentionally seek a second slap. We stand firm in offering God's love to the world, willing to love at the risk of our other cheek. When turning the other cheek, we don't act passively. We take an active position of choosing to persevere in love. Only in Christ do we find this miraculous love that is unfailing. With this genuine love, we can always welcome others properly to Christ . . .

The Welcome Mat

The saying, "I'm not a doormat!" or "God didn't call me to be a doormat!" is a saying that means, "Don't step on me to get where you're going." But one day when I became upset about something I made this statement and the Spirit whispered into my heart:

"No, but you are not the Door, either."

Jesus is the Door. No one can enter heaven except through Jesus. Again I heard the whispers, "Donna, are you willing to be a doormat if I call you to be one?" In my mind I could see a welcome mat—the kind that sits in front of a door. The mat cannot replace the door. The mat welcomes all who come to the door. God doesn't always call us to be a doormat to assist others to the door, but if He does—are we willing?

By listening to the Spirit of God we can know when we need to remove ourselves from a situation, or whether He has called us to be a "spiritual doormat" in this situation. When an angry crowd wanted to stone Jesus, He knew it wasn't God's will for that to happen, so He slipped away. But we also know of a time when He went willingly to a Cross to become the sacrificial lamb for us—knowing that this *was* the will of the Father. If we are faithful to follow the will of the Father, we will receive the blessing promised to the one who overcomes: "Be faithful until death, and I will give you the crown of life . . . He who overcomes shall not be hurt by the second death" (Revelation 2:10b, 11b).

Overcoming can mean victory over our own self-will, or it can mean victory over situations that could tempt us to deny our faith. When we overcome self-will, we become victorious in offering Christ's love. Christ's love is the miraculous bread that remains tender, compassionate, and unfailing. Jesus said, "My Father gives you the true bread from heaven. For the bread of God is He who comes down from heaven and gives life to the world . . . I am the bread of life" (John 6:32b, 33, 35a).

Jesus is the Bread of Life. When we die daily to circumstances that tempt us to respond with temperamental emotions and self-ish motives, we allow the Bread of Life to increase in our lives. But what happens if instead of allowing Christ to increase in our lives we become fooled by thinking that our own love is good enough . . . ?

Fooled by Our Own Good Works

After teaching about God's love to a Bible study group, my friend Le, who is known for her good cooking, approached me. She told me to add a bit of sugar to the yeast the next time I baked bread, because it would boost the yeast's performance. Adding sugar to the yeast sounded like a good idea. It's like adding a little "insurance" to the dough so the loaves always turn out perfect! The Lord whispered to my heart about the (supposedly) perfect loaves that contain sugar. Sugar tastes sweet, but it lacks real nutrition. It fools our taste buds into thinking we are eating something good when we actually aren't.

Adding sugar is like using those popular false teachings, which advocate ideas that sound good and feel good. Many times, such false teachings add vain philosophies of works or human effort to make us feel better about ourselves. This reminds me of what Jesus said in this next Scripture to the Pharisees who thought they were good because of their works:

> For you are like whitewashed tombs which indeed appear beautiful outwardly, but inside are full of dead *men's* bones and all uncleanness. Even so you also outwardly appear righteous to men, but inside you are full of hypocrisy and lawlessness. (Matthew 23:27b, 28)

It seems easier whitewashing ourselves with false appearances of love than for us to die to self so we can love with Christ's love. This whitewashing with false appearances is like putting sugary frosting on my hard, dry, and tasteless loaves. They may look good, but on the inside the bread would remain hard, dry, and tasteless. No matter what we *add* to our love, it's still like the sugarcoated loaf that contains only "empty calories." We may look good on the outside, but because of our sinful nature, the inside still contains death and destruction. One of the ways we can whitewash with false appearances, thinking we're looking good, is through a popular false teaching on unconditional love.

Now unconditional love is very real. It is the love Jesus expressed to us when He died on the Cross. This love is not based on our behavior or anything about us, but on the Lord's great mercy toward us. Even when we were still sinners, undeserving of His love, God showed His unconditional love to mankind by giving His life for us. Unconditional love was God reaching out to us, even while we still lived in our sins.

However, this exceptional love doesn't mean God is willing to accept our continuing to willfully sin. Rather, God made a way to cleanse us from our sins so that we could fellowship with Him. God loves us so much He paid the price to remove our sin. But the false teaching of unconditional love says that if God loves us unconditionally there are no consequences for sin. This causes many to stumble, thinking they can live as they please, continuing to sin without regard to God. The Lord whispered into my heart to give me further understanding about unconditional love and the consequences of sin. He asked me to consider a good father's love for his children.

When a father loves his children, he wants the best for them. If his children seek ways that will ultimately cause harm to themselves or others, the father responds by providing negative consequences to correct their behavior. But if the father believes that unconditional love means he must not offer any consequences for bad behavior, the child will be very unruly. Ultimately the false teaching of unconditional love—or sin with no consequences—results in unfruitful lives for the uncorrected child and causes embarrassment for the father. To bring up his children without consequences can never provide an example of unconditional paternal love; rather, it shows a father's laziness or even his lack of love. It is out of the good father's love for his children that he disciplines them to correct their bad behaviors.

As a good parent, God does the same with us. He wants the best for us. He is not an abusive Father; He truly loves us and wants us to enjoy fruitful lives. So when we behave in rebellion to Him, in ways that ultimately cause harm to others, or ourselves the Word says He disciplines us. He reproves us and makes the effort of a good Father to set us straight. Ahh, but then it's the choice of the child of God to respond in either obedience or rebellion—just as it is with *our* children. Ultimately we must make the decision about how we will respond to God's reproof, not only in actions and attitude, but even more importantly—in the heart.

If we believe that unconditional love means God is unconcerned about our sins and loves us too much to reprove us—we will be whitewashing ourselves with a false teaching. This teaching sounds good and feels good but, just like sugar, it's false and unhealthy.

To love others with an unconditional love that holds forth no consequences for sin is also phony. Such "love" is much like sugar—it may be sweet, but it lacks real value. It can fool our hearts into thinking we are receiving something good when we're not. This false teaching motivates us to treat others with a syrupy kind of love that isn't real—like the frosting on my hard, dry, and tasteless loaves—yuck! Real love must be tough sometimes. Like the good father's love, sometimes it's tough because it cares and loves enough to set consequences. This love is sincere, and its sweetness is pure—not doctored up with empty, sugary frosting.

Although sugar can be a good "insurance" for the baker so his bread baking will turn out well, there is no similar insurance in us. Unlike the procedure with bread dough, we can't add any *insurance* to our sinful nature that will make a life without Christ turn out well. Our love will just never do as well as His. We can only insure that we're loving others properly through Christ when we choose to *die to self* daily. Then we can respond as a vessel filled with the Bread of Life's unfailing love . . .

The Vessel

One night the Holy Spirit directed my attention to what the clay bowl in my hand contained: popcorn sprinkled with salt. I didn't understand what the Spirit was telling me at that moment, except that I knew that the clay bowl represents us. Later that same evening, when the entire contents of the bowl fell on the floor, the whispers of the Holy Spirit were clearly understood when I heard these two Scriptures:

1. Knowledge puffs up, but love edifies (1 Corinthians 8:1b).

2. Pride *goes* before destruction, And a haughty spirit before a fall (Proverbs 16:18).

Popcorn filled the clay bowl with only a trace of salt sprinkled on top. *What do the popcorn and salt represent?* I wondered.

Popcorn and Salt

Salt in the Scriptures generally symbolizes that special ingredient Christians possess which helps them to affect the world around them. Salt is a preservative, which keeps meat from rotting; a seasoning that flavors; and a healer that cleanses wounds deeply. As Christians, we use our "saltiness" to preserve others from the rotting effects of sin; to season the world by enhancing, rather than becoming just like the world; and to reach deeply into the hearts of the broken and oppressed . . . bringing healing.

When we puff up dry kernels of corn with hot air, we get popcorn—symbolic of someone who is "puffed up" with pride or "hot air." The popcorn sprinkled with salt in the clay bowl symbolizes a believer who is puffed up with prideful knowledge, seeking to affect the world with a sprinkling of his own abilities. Knowledge is a good thing, yet when it becomes puffed up, it's ugly. As we see from the Scriptures above, knowledge doesn't offer anything of lasting value, while *love* does. And what a waste of salt! Sprinkling it on puffed-up, prideful knowledge that doesn't edify!

When we are puffed up with prideful knowledge, we too will fall—just as my clay bowl fell scattering its contents. This fall symbolizes the trials we go through to purify us, or in this case—to empty us of self. When we empty our vessels of self, which offers only empty, meaningless "hot air," we can seek instead to become filled with God's salty love. Then the world will taste our saltiness and know we are His because: "By this all will know that you are My disciples, if you have love for one another" (John 13:35).

It is through our love for others that the world will know we belong to Jesus. To live as the salt of the earth, we need to empty ourselves of our popcorn (prideful knowledge), and then die to self with our "temperamental yeast" (our own love with its sinful nature). We must do this without adding any "sugary frosting" (false appearances / whitewashing), and seek to offer only God's love to others. Then we will love the world with the true Bread of Life's unfailing love and indeed be the salt of the earth!

My Prayer:

Lord, remove the temperamental yeast from me, and help me to love others with Your love, which is enduring and not temperamental. Help me to die to self, with my natural responses, which prefer to duck from injury or strike back at others. Then help me to stand firm in offering Your love to others, even if You call me to turn the other cheek or—sometimes, to fulfill Your purposes—to be a "spiritual doormat." Amen.

We can offer Christ's love to others (and to ourselves) better when we understand how much God values life. How much does God value life? How do painful trials cause us to value life less? What are the opinions of the world that can cause us to devalue life . . . ?

SEVEN
God Values Life

Lord, You are the Creator of life.
It's precious at every stage,
From the tiny babe within the womb,
To the white-haired elder sage.

WHAT CAUSES US TO DEVALUE LIFE? AS I PONDERED THIS QUESTION, GOD whispered to me.

Life's a Bummer and Then You Die?

While my friend Debby stood sharing her testimony, many of us decided to re-think the value we placed on life. Being unaware of Debby's difficult past before accepting Christ, we had always assumed this beautiful career woman had lived the ideal life. Yet here she stood—talking of sad, broken relationships, drugs, close encounters with death, jail, and hopelessness. A drastically different life than what we now saw before us! She told us how Jesus taught her to value life because He valued her. To paraphrase my friend's words, she said, "Life's not a bummer and then you die. Life is precious. Jesus gave up His earthly life so that we could have eternal life with Him. Although we live in a fallen world full of sin, we can live victoriously and in peace . . . for our faith isn't of this world or the things in it, but our faith is in our Father in heaven."

While pondering Debby's testimony, the Lord whispered in my heart, teaching me how He values life. Then the Lord made me aware of other elements in everyday living that can cause the believer to lower the value we place on life. Of course, sin devalues life because it leads to death, but so can painful trials and worldly opinions. First, how can painful trials cause us to value life less . . . ?

Painful Trials

My friend Skip almost died in a serious car accident. While he lay in a hospital barely holding on to life, many people prayed for him. He survived, but spent a long time in rehabilitation because the accident had left him paralyzed. When I visited Skip periodically through the years that followed, I could see in his face that he was angry and that he devalued his life because of this painful trial. Alternately, there were times when he shined with the love of Jesus so strongly that it was obvious he not only loved and valued his life, but also loved and valued the lives of others.

Several years had passed since I'd visited with this friend. Then one Sunday evening, as my mother and I sat in the back of a large church we attended, the Spirit whispered into my heart: "Tell your mother that tonight I will show you both that I answered your prayers."

To hear the Spirit's voice is great. But when He tells me to repeat it to someone else, this definitely tests my faith! I couldn't shake the words in my heart, so I turned and whispered in her ear what I heard. She looked at me and, as her eyebrows narrowed, said, "Huh?" I decided it really wasn't too risky for your own mother to think you're strange—she's expected to love you anyway, right? So I told her again.

Thankfully it didn't take long to see exactly what the Spirit had meant. The pastor called our congregation's Bible college graduates forward to receive their diplomas. My friend Skip, sitting in his wheelchair, was among them! Mother and I cried for joy. We had both prayed for him frequently. That night I also met his beautiful wife, Anne. Since the writing of this book, Skip received a promotion to academic dean of a Bible college in Southern California. God loves and values this man so much, He had a plan for his life that continued beyond his fierce trial. God loves and values each of us so much that He has a plan for our lives, too. My friend achieved victory over his painful trial because of his faith in the Creator of life. I'm sure he still faces moments of weakness, as we all do. Yet we can live in true peace as we learn to trust God with all of our life.

Painful trials tempt us to focus on the circumstances instead of the Lord. Pain alone can provoke us to anger and ultimately cause us to value life less. When we find ourselves in the midst of a difficult trial, we must maintain our focus on Jesus—trusting Him with our lives. This is a daily decision. If the trial intensifies, we may even struggle moment by moment. Yet even in those times we can trust God, because He promised not to allow any temptation to try us beyond what we can endure, as this Scripture promises: "God *is* faithful, who will not allow you to be tempted beyond what you are able, but with the temptation will also make the way of escape, that you may be able to bear *it*" (1 Corinthians 10:13b). While painful trials tempt us to value life less, even so do worldly opinions.

Worldly Opinions

The Lord whispered a warning to me of five worldly opinions of which we should always be aware. We must seek truth actively, rejecting any opinion that disagrees with the Word. Of course, these five are not the only opinions that devalue life; they are just the ones the Lord whispered into my heart in the lesson He was teaching me.

When we want to know truth, we must learn to challenge opinions—especially those that cause us to value God's good gift of life less. These five worldly opinions can serve as examples to stir our minds to consider other opinions that may subtly sway our values. The first worldly opinion, and probably the most overlooked until we reach old age, concerns the treatment of older people.

First Opinion: On Old Age

In American culture we place a higher value on staying young than on growing old. When we treat the older generation with disrespect, it gives them a feeling of uselessness at a time in their lives when they've earned respect and honor for their years and wisdom. We miss a blessing by not seeking wisdom from our seniors, especially from older Christians who have known the Lord longer than we ourselves. What does God say about how to treat the older generation? "You shall give due honor and respect to the elderly, in the fear of God. I am Jehovah" (Leviticus 19:32 TLB). We value older people best when we give them the honor and respect due to them.

Second Opinion: On Television Programming

Sometime during the 1960s we entered the "age of television." Now, while this household appliance is not in itself evil, what comes into our living rooms through it on the airwaves can be. Devaluing of human life happens in various ways through TV programs and movies, but mostly through a constant barrage of scenes of violence. By watching this violence continually, we grow desensitized to human pain. The Word of God lists sins (described as evils) that range from disobedience in children to murder. At the end of the long Scripture in Romans describing these evils is a declaration that causes the believer to note that, "Although they know God's righteous decree that those who do such things deserve death, they not only continue to do these very things *but also approve of those who practice them*" (Romans 1:32 NIV, emphasis is author's).

When we watch TV, we approve of and take pleasure in whatever we allow to entertain us. Pray and ask the Spirit of Truth to reveal to you what things devalue life and displease God. We have a great promise that He will guide us into all truth.

Third Opinion: On the Theory of Evolution

In today's society, most people accept the Theory of Evolution as a fact. Evolution teaches that we evolved from amino acids, which spontaneously combined over billions of years to form human life, and that we're just one of many species going through a process. Although Charles Darwin himself admitted that the universe had to have been conceived by a divine mind, his theory, as it is taught in schools today, frequently denies that a God of creation exists at all! If we accept this theory of Evolution, life offers no hope for the future since it implies there is no purpose for human life beyond that of any other animal continuing to evolve into the unknown.

The Word tells us what will happen if we choose not to believe in the God of creation. Romans, Chapter Three says that we'll have no excuse when we stand before God, because even creation declares there is a God. God created us in His image and breathed life into man and woman, giving them dominion over all living things on earth. We didn't evolve from animals; God created us for His good pleasure. With Him, we have hope and a peace about our future.

Fourth Opinion: On the Right-to-Take-a-Life

In 1973 American courts granted a woman the right to choose whether her unborn child would be considered a baby or fetus . . . life, or tissue. Life and death for the unborn began, from that moment, to depend greatly upon her individual opinion. But the Word says God formed and fashioned each one of us in our mother's womb and that He knew us before we were born! (Note: If you *have* been involved in an abortion and repented, God has forgiveness for you. My Prayer: Lord, I pray for anyone who may read this who's been involved in an abortion. I pray that You will forgive them, and allow them to feel Your great and merciful love.)

Fifth Opinion: On Death and the Occult

Taking a walk through any music store today, we can catch a glimpse of the enormous interest in the worship and adoration of death and the occult. The covers of many recordings depict death and occult imagery; the two go hand in hand. Just as Jesus represents and brings life, Satan represents and brings death. When people choose to worship the occult and Satan's demons, it always points to death and human destruction. An anonymous writer once wrote, "Earth is the best heaven a sinner will ever know, and the worst hell a believer will ever endure."

Worshipping the devil and his angels leads only to death and destruction. Jesus came to extend our lives—not shorten them. This Scripture portrays God's great love and the value He holds for the entire world: "For God so loved the world that He gave His only begotten Son, that whoever believes in Him should not perish but have everlasting life" (John 3:16).

God Values Life

We can clearly see God's opinion of life in Genesis, Chapter One, when after creating everything He said it was "very good." Even after we sinned against God and the world suffered because of it, God didn't give up on us. He revealed His great love for us by showing how much He valued us, even when we were still sinners. What can separate us from the love of God now?

Who shall separate us from the love of Christ? . . . For I am persuaded that neither death nor life, nor angels nor principalities nor powers, nor things present nor things to come, nor height nor depth, nor any other created thing, shall be able to separate us from the love of God which is in Christ Jesus our Lord. (Romans 8:35a, 38, 39)

God values each of us so much that He refuses to let anything separate us from Him! God values us, and He gave us a precious gift called life! We need to value our lives. If we fail to value life as God intended we most likely will fail to value the children of our world. But how does God want us to value the children He's placed among us . . . ?

The Promise of a Rose

During a time in my life when I struggled with painful trials, I had a dream. In the dream, the Lord not only revealed to me the reason for the trials, but also communicated that He desired to give me a blessing. When I awoke, I knew the Lord used this dream to whisper into my heart—and the meaning of the dream was clear. Have you noticed that I'm not always the mature, accepting, willing vessel I should be? Hopefully this will encourage you, as you see that God doesn't give up on any of us easily. Praise God! My response to God's blessing:

"Oh, great! I know what a blessing is to You, God—a baby! I'm tired, and right now I don't see how that's supposed to help!" Sure enough, I was pregnant. Before the birth I told my sister Irene that she could name the baby if it was a girl. (Dan and I had run out of girls' names!) Irene was so excited she prayed to the Lord for help with this awesome responsibility. As we drove up to Irene's home, she ran out the front door and announced:

"I found a name, Donna! Kimberly! And since Dan wants the middle name to be Rose after his grandmother, it would be Kimberly Rose."

"That's a nice name, Irene. Do you know what it means?" I asked.

"No, but I'll find out!" Irene discovered the meaning right away. I didn't think her excitement could grow stronger, but when she returned she could hardly contain herself.

"Kimberly means 'from the royal fortress.' So her name would mean 'from the royal fortress, a rose.' And since God is in *the* royal fortress, I believe her name means God has given you a rose!"

The Spirit whispered into my heart, reminding me of the dream of a promised blessing. A few months later we held our blessing in our arms: Kimberly Rose Fitzpatrick—a rose that will never fade since we intend to spend eternity with her. The Lord not only fulfilled His promise to me of a blessing, but also began to teach me more about the little "Roses."

Little Devils or Little Angels?

Because I have several children, I'm often asked, "Why did you bring another child into this corrupt and evil world?" This question implies that children are little angels facing sure destruction by a hopelessly evil world. So, why continue this thing called life? Another question that I frequently hear is: "Wow, how many children do you have? You must be a saint!" This implies that children are burdensome little devils. So why would anyone want children? Both of these statements reveal a questionable attitude of the heart. But what does God say our attitudes should be toward children?

What Does the Word Say About Children?

God desires that we value children as a blessing—not devalue them like burdensome little devils, or esteem them too highly, like little angels. If we would compare a child to anything, a rose seems quite fitting since it's a package deal. The rose not only has a sweet smell, but also prickly thorns. The sweet aroma compares to a child's innocence, while the thorns remind us of the child's inborn ability to sin.

Roses require water, food, pruning, and love to grow well. Children require the same elements to thrive. We tend to the children of our world, taking care not to lead them astray. Jesus loves all children; He told us so. Our children are the next generation; it's important that we value them the way God does. Children, like my little Kimberly Rose, are precious gifts from God:

Behold, children *are* a heritage from the Lord, The fruit of the womb *is* a reward. Like arrows in the hand of a warrior, So *are* the children of one's youth. Happy *is* the man who has his quiver full of them. (Psalms 127:3–5a)

Yes, children are a blessing! We must always remember to value them and the life He's given us.

My Prayer:

Thank You, God, for my earthly life and for the eternal life You've given me! Thank You for the elderly. Teach me how to show them honor and respect. Thank You for valuing me before I was even born. Thank You for television, which can show me many good things. Help me to use it in a way that brings honor to You and respect for life as You created it. Help me to love others, including the children I meet, as You do, and help me to value the life You've given me. And thank You, Lord, that Your love is not limited to a select few, but is vast, not limited to one time, one nation, or one age.

Blessed be Your glorious name, Which is exalted above all blessing and praise! You alone are the Lord; You have made heaven,
The heaven of heavens, with all their host, The earth and everything on it, The seas and all that is in them, And You preserve
them all. The host of heaven worships You. (Nehemiah 9:5b, 6)

Amen.

༄   ༄   ༄

*One of the most important spiritual lessons we can share with
our children is how to yield ourselves to God—to become a
broken vessel for His use. But what is a broken vessel? How
do we become broken, and what attitudes prevent us from
being broken . . . ?*

EIGHT

Broken to Be Made Whole

You are a useful vessel,
Fallen upon the Stone.
Yes, you are broken . . . now of good use
To Him who sits on the throne.

WHY IS IT IMPORTANT TO BE BROKEN? AND WHAT ATTITUDES PREVENT US from being so?

The Clay Vessel

While cleaning the kitchen table, I picked up the centerpiece fruit bowl and wiped beneath it. Suddenly I felt a strong impression that it would soon be broken. Now this particular fruit bowl had adorned the table for several years; there was no logical reason why I felt it should break now. I didn't realize then that this very impression was itself another whisper of the Holy Spirit.

Yet the impression was so strong that I began searching for a spot in a cupboard to hide the bowl in an attempt to prevent it from being broken. I located a safe cupboard, but just when I set it on the highest shelf a feeling of foolishness swept over me. Why, this bowl had been purchased for the express purpose of offering beautiful fruit to my family for nourishment. By hiding the bowl, no one would enjoy the beauty, nor the nutrition from the fruit it held. So back to the table it went, come-what-may. I later discovered that my feeling of not wanting to hide the bowl was yet another whisper from the Holy Spirit. Very soon the Lord used these two whispers to teach me a foundational truth in His Word.

Two days later, while washing the breakfast dishes, I heard a loud crash behind me. Turning around, I saw my bowl—broken in a million small pieces, which danced and whirled around the floor. Looking somewhat sheepish, my husband Dan stood near the scattered pieces of the beloved fruit bowl. I just couldn't be angry with him. Not because he was overtly sorry, but because of the quiet impression I had received only a few days prior . . . So, I just stood there in awe and wonder while I watched in silence and asked the Lord what this meant. Dan kindly swept up the pieces and threw them away.

The Vessel Had to be Broken

In the Old Testament, when a person offered a sacrifice for his sins, this sinner placed his hands on the sacrificial animal's head. This signified that the animal was taking on the sins of the person bringing the sacrifice. Then the person killed the animal and the priests offered it to the Lord. Yet the sacrifice of the animal could not fully remove the sin; it could only cover it. That's why these sacrifices did not fulfill the law and needed to be repeated.

After the priest cooked the sacrificial meat in a clay vessel, Mosaic Law (Old Testament law) required that the bowl had to be broken. Although the priests broke the bowl in obedience to these laws, we now see that the bowl was broken because it represented Christ. An interesting fact about clay vessels is that they are porous. Porous simply means that whatever is put into the vessel remains in the pores of the clay even after the vessel is washed. So this vessel, that represented Christ, contained holiness deep in its pores. In fact, it was, and is thoroughly holy.

All of us are similar to clay vessels, but unlike this holy vessel, our vessels contain sin. No matter how many times we try to rid ourselves of sin, we find that—as the children of Adam—sin is embedded deep in our hearts. Because of this sin, we face eternal separation from God or spiritual death. But God desires fellowship with us so much that He offered us His redeeming plan. If we accept this plan, our vessels will contain Christ's perfect sacrifice, making *us* holy unto God. But what must we do to receive the perfect sacrifice?

The Perfect Sacrifice

We cannot earn salvation. Nor can we ever be good enough to earn acceptance with God. For this reason, Jesus became the perfect sacrificial lamb. He contained no sin, so death could not hold Him captive for any crime. Because God provided the perfect sacrifice, we are free from the law, which required that "The soul who sins shall die" (Ezekiel 18:4b). It's not that the law against sin was done away with; rather, that Jesus fulfilled its demand of "death to all sinners" by dying Himself in our place. Being the "perfect sacrifice," He gave His life once—for all. Nevertheless, to receive this sacrifice for our sins, we must do what the Scripture tells us, and be broken for, "Whoever falls on that stone will be broken; but on whomever it falls, it will grind him to powder" (Luke 20:18). Jesus is this Stone.

Christ's body was broken because of man's sin. For this sin we deserve death. But because Jesus was broken in our place, God can offer us a choice: we can acknowledge Christ's sacrificial brokenness and fall on Him by repenting—being broken—or we can refuse to do so. If we refuse to be broken in humble acknowledgment of Christ, we will face the Stone on Judgment Day. The stone will fall on us, and "grind us to powder," a dramatic symbol of eternal separation from God.

If we choose to fall on the rock through repentance, we give our lives to Christ and invite Him to rule over our hearts. Then, because our human vessel will now hold the perfect sacrifice within it, He does the miraculous! He takes our unclean, broken vessel and makes it clean and whole again. In these two Scriptures, we first see how Jesus makes us clean, then how wonderfully He restores us to wholeness:

1. **The Lord Cleanses Us:**
   Though your sins are like scarlet, They shall be as white as snow; Though they are red like crimson, They shall be as wool (Isaiah 1:18b).

2. **The Lord Heals Our Brokenness:**
   But for you who revere my name, the sun of righteousness will rise with healing in its wings. And you will go out and leap like calves released from the stall (Malachi 4:2 NIV).

Calves from the Stall

The Lord is saying in this last verse that after He heals us, we'll feel like a calf released from its stall! To understand this joyous release, picture a young boy kept in all day . . . looking out the window, watching friends at play, yearning to join them with every inch of his little body. When the door finally opens to let the child out—we can easily visualize his reaction—running, jumping, and shouting!

The calf in our Scripture is in a worse situation. He lives in a dark stall that leaves him hardly enough room to turn around. Then one day someone releases the calf from his confining stall. The door flies open and, with a burst of excitement, he finds himself outside in a grassy meadow—running, jumping, and shaking off the smell of the stall while drinking in deep breaths of fresh, clean air.

A similar but worse situation is the man or woman, boy or girl in bondage to sin. This one cannot escape the tight grip of sin that holds his spirit, soul, and body, and the foul odor of death. The amazing thing is that the door has already been unlocked. All we need do is to be broken (repent) to go through the doorway from bondage to freedom. Jesus is that door. And in fact, there is no other way to be saved but through Him. Freedom! It's there for the taking. But if we can *all* experience this freedom, why are some people *unwilling* to be broken? Rebellion.

Repentance or Rebellion?—Broken or Unbroken?

Rebellion is doing anything disobedient to what God desires. The Holy Spirit whispers to each of our hearts—drawing us to Jesus. When the Spirit shines the Lord's perfect light in our hearts and exposes all of the darkness of sin, we make a conscious choice: repentance or rebellion? Even when we refuse to choose Christ, our failure to choose reveals our choice since Jesus told us, "He who is not with Me is against Me" (Matthew 12:30a).

Thus if we are not coming forth for Jesus Christ, we stand against Him. If we do not repent of our disobedience to God, we are living in rebellion toward Him. When we choose to rebel, the Word says we will face judgment and eternal separation from God. Here are four common mindsets that reveal rebellious attitudes against God:

1. Not Admitting to Sin: Unbroken

The person with this mindset says, "I'm OK, and you're OK!" If we hold this attitude, we don't see a need for God. We would be unwilling to see any serious imperfections in our lives, or we simply accept them. If we're truly "OK," Jesus didn't need to come to earth and take the form of man, live a perfect, spotless life, die on the Cross for our sins, then rise on the third day. But He did, because we're not "OK." This Scripture tells us why: "For all have sinned and fall short of the glory of God" (Romans 3:23). We have *all* sinned and we all need our Savior, Jesus Christ, to make us "OK" in God's sight.

2. Admitting of Sin / Will Fix Self: Unbroken

The person with this mindset says, "Yes, I see imperfection or sin in my life, but I'll fix myself up, thank you. We all have a good and evil side; I just need to concentrate more on my good side. I can do it if I try hard enough and think good thoughts."

If we hold this attitude we might be willing to *admit* to our sin, but we'd also believe that our goodness alone is enough to solve the problem of sin. This Scripture gives us a picture of what our goodness or righteousness is like: "But we are all like an unclean *thing*, And all our righteousnesses *are* like filthy rags" (Isaiah 64:6a).

These weren't just dirty rags; they were gross and smelly. So completely disgusting no one wanted to even look at them. Our own goodness is just like these rags; we can never clean ourselves up enough for God to accept us. We need Jesus to cleanse us from our sin.

3. Admitting Sin / Yet Accepting Sin: Unbroken

The person with this mindset says, "Yes, I sin, but no one's perfect. I like myself, and at least I'm honest with myself."

This kind of "honesty" doesn't solve the problem of sin. It simply opens the closet door to "air it." If we hold this attitude of admitting our sin without repenting of it, it would appear that we don't believe in God or in His coming judgment. This Scripture foretells the coming judgment and what we will be doing at it:

For it is written: *"As I live, says the Lord,*
Every knee shall bow to Me,
And every tongue shall confess to God."
So then each of us shall give account
of himself to God. (Romans 14:11, 12)

Again we see—we need our Savior.

4. Admitting Sin / Repenting / Yet No Change in Life: Broken?

The person with this mindset says, "Sure, I'm a religious person. Now that I know my sins are forgiven, I can live as I please!"

The following Scripture depicts this religious person very well. *Hold on to your stomach!*

For if, after they have escaped the pollutions of the world through the knowledge of the Lord and Savior Jesus Christ, they are again entangled in them and overcome, the latter end is worse for them than the beginning. For it would have been better for them not to have known the way of righteousness, than having known *it*, to turn from the holy commandment delivered to them. But it has happened to them according to the true proverb: *"A dog returns to his own vomit,"* and, "a sow, having washed, to her wallowing in the mire." (2 Peter 2:20–22)

If we boast of this attitude to the Cross of Jesus it may mean that we simply became "religious." We would be merely giving lip service of accepting Christ, but never making a heartfelt decision. But what is the right response to the Cross of Jesus?

5. Admitting / Repenting: Broken

The person with this mindset says, "Yes, Jesus, I fall on you. You are my rock of salvation. I am a sinner, and I need Your forgiveness. Break my rebellion and help me to live a life of obedience to You."

In this next Scripture we see what we need to do to receive for-giveness of our sins: "If we confess our sins, He is faithful and just to forgive us *our* sins and to cleanse us from all unrighteousness" (1 John 1:9). Yes! We first need Jesus to forgive our sins and cleanse us. Yet even after we accept Christ's salvation we can take on one of the four mindsets of unbrokenness (above) that says:

1. "I'm OK. *I don't need* to be made whole."
2. "*I can fix* my broken vessel."
3. "*I don't want* to change."
4. "*I'm free* to live as I please."

We make choices every day whether to serve self or to submit to God's will for our lives. All of the above mindsets are in rebel-lion to God. When we let our hearts become hard and bitter from such unbroken attitudes, which serve self, the soil in our souls can become as hard and thorny as the fallow ground described below.

Fallow Ground

Fallow ground is an uncultivated field—a field where something should be growing, but nothing is. What happened? The thorny weeds grew, unchecked, instead. The Lord says, "Break up your fallow ground, And do not sow among thorns. Circumcise your-selves to the Lord, And take away the foreskins of your hearts" (Jeremiah 4:3b, 4a).

The Lord says break up the hard ground, pull the weeds out and prepare for the planting and the harvest to follow. Similar to the way in which fallow ground turns hard and thorny without the care of a gardener, our hearts turn hard and bitter without the touch of Jesus. Jesus never neglects us; rather, we become self-sufficient or return to the sinful life. Fallow ground, without the touch of Jesus, cannot offer anything nutritious—only empty thorns. Just so our hearts, without the touch of the Lord, cannot sow or reap righteousness. The Word says, "Sow for yourselves righteousness; Reap in mercy; Break up your fallow ground, For *it is* time to seek the Lord, Till He comes and rains righteousness on you" (Hosea 10:12).

It is time to seek the Lord. If the soil of our hearts has turned hard and unfruitful, we need to break up the hardness of our hearts so that He can "rain righteousness" in our lives. Sadly, pride often gets in the way, causing us to remain hard-hearted or self-righteous, rather than embracing the humble heart required to receive the righteousness of Christ.

Self-Righteous—*Versus*—Righteous Through Christ

In this present age there is a preoccupation with the desire to "be better." If the desire is self-centered rather than Christ-centered, it isn't good. It may cause us, as believers, to center our thoughts on self, our fleshly dreams, or brokenness. Focusing on our brokenness is uncomfortable to our pride. Being uncomfortable, we may seek worldly ways to try to repair our brokenness. This doesn't please God. When we focus on self by believing we can repair our own brokenness through good works, we merely achieve self-righteousness—not the righteousness of Christ.

Actually, we obtain righteousness only through obedience and faith in Christ. Since the time when we received Christ and died to self by falling on the rock, we know that faithful Jesus will continue to chip away at any areas in our lives that remain in rebellion to Him. Remember, there are only two ways to respond when Jesus reveals sin in our lives: repentance or rebellion. Through the healing touch of Christ's nail-scarred hands, He makes us whole and clean. Truly our righteousness is *only* through Christ. Clothed with His righteousness, we become a vessel of honor for Him.

Useful Vessel of Honor

Remember when I started to hide my bowl in the cupboard? We don't belong in a cupboard! As surely as an unclean man in shackles, we've been set free from bondage. When we ask the Lord to break any areas in our lives that are still in rebellion to Him, He won't throw us away like my fruit bowl. This is what Jesus will do with us: "Therefore if anyone cleanses himself from the latter, he will be a vessel for honor, sanctified and useful for the Master, prepared for every good work" (2 Timothy 2:21).

Working miraculously, Jesus molds us into vessels of honor He uses to offer the fruits of the Spirit. Just as I purchased my fruit bowl to offer fresh fruit to my family, the precious blood of Jesus purchased us—and we, too, will offer fruit to others. My bowl contained only temporal fruit, however, while our vessels contain spiritual fruit that will last for eternity. "But the fruit of the Spirit is love, joy, peace, longsuffering, kindness, goodness, faithfulness, gentleness, self-control" (Galatians 5:22). Our vessels hold an abundance of fruit to share with a hungry world. But before we can be implanted with the seeds of these nine fruits, we must fall on the Rock, and the fallow ground of our hearts must be broken, bringing cleansing from the thorny weeds of sin. If you haven't yet asked Jesus to be your Lord and you feel the whisperings of the Holy Spirit tugging at your heart right now, you can say a prayer something like this:

> Jesus, I believe You are the only begotten Son of the Father. You died for me on the Cross so that my sins could be forgiven. Please forgive me of my sins. Come into my heart so I may have eternal life with You. Amen.

If you prayed this prayer to God by faith in Jesus, you now have eternal life with Him and all of His people. Now you can look forward to experiencing the growth *process* toward wholeness implemented by our Savior! The Lord whispered more to me about this process through a home my husband Dan built in Oakland, California . . .

Spiritual Houses

Dan built a house on a hilltop overlooking San Francisco, which developed problems in completion. This house replaced a first home, which had burned down in the Oakland, California fire of 1990. Even before the groundbreaking of the project, a neighbor complained that the new house was going to stand too close to his property. As the neighbors argued and engineers differed in their findings, it was finally decided that the proposed house *did* need to be moved over. Other neighbors complained the house would block their view. There seemed to be no solution to this problem. Unless the owner had his house built underground, this complaint would remain unsettled!

Dan worked outdoors in rain and hard winds. He started early and worked till late into the night. As he worked, he found more problems—and eventually solved them all. One problem originated from the house plans, which hadn't considered the steep slope in the front portion of the building lot. To solve the problem, Dan built a long, beautiful set of stairs to the main entrance. The troubles were many but, when Dan finally finished, the owner expressed great pleasure with the result of his beautiful new home.

The Lord whispered to my heart showing me that you and I are like this house. The Master Builder, Jesus, is building us. Our original house died with Jesus on the Cross—when we accepted Him into our hearts—just as the original home here had burned down in the massive fire. Our new house is still in the rebuilding process. While in this process, we still have free will. Free will means we can choose to be obedient to our Master Builder, or to be rebellious. Obedience makes the Builder's job quicker and less painful, while rebellion causes problems and lengthens the building process.

In our times of rebellion we need to move over—just as the exact location of the Oakland house moved. These are times when we are broken by repenting and requesting forgiveness. Then there are times when people persecute us, but we can only stand. Just as the Oakland house still stands even though neighbors complained of it blocking their view. The only thing we can do during times of persecution is try to be as transparent as we can be so that these critical people see Jesus and repent of their judgments. Remember the necessary changes Dan made to the front of the house?—the long set of stairs he designed to compensate for the steep slope in the front entry. This change probably made the house look quite different from the one the homeowner had originally imagined. Sometimes we imagine ourselves differently than our Master Builder views us. We don't need to fear these differences in His plan. We can trust the Master's touch in our lives, knowing He has good plans for us. In those areas in which we are weak, He will make us strong. He specializes in building strong spiritual houses that will last for eternity.

Because the Lord isn't finished with us we need to be obedient to His work. We must be ready to forgive wrong judgments as well as to request forgiveness when we've overstepped our boundaries. Best of all, this Scripture makes us a beautiful promise: "Being confident of this very thing, that He who has begun a good work in you will complete *it* until the day of Jesus Christ" (Philippians 1:6).

We can look forward to this day of completion!

My Prayer:

Lord, forgive my rebellion. Help me yield to Your hand as You turn this vessel into a vessel of honor that offers others Your fruit. For You are the Potter, and I am the clay. Keep me humble to see my brokenness and wise to know that You're the one that makes me whole. And thank you Lord for Your promise to complete the work You started in me. Help me to surrender to Your touch while the work is in progress, and encourage my heart to know that, though I may make mistakes, *I* am not a mistake. Amen.

❧   ❧   ❧

We maintain an attitude of brokenness so the Lord can make us whole. But what are the materials used to build our spiritual houses? Have we built with wood, hay, and straw—or with gold and silver? And what is the only foundation that will keep our houses secure . . . ?

Nine

A Matter of Security

Building alone using wood, hay, or straw,
Brings insecurity, awaiting a fall.
Building with Christ using silver and gold,
Brings true security as faith takes hold!

WHAT BRINGS INSECURITY AND FALSE SECURITY? WHAT CAN WE BUILD ON that will bring true security?

The Rusty Nut

Dan was helping a neighbor build his house, and, since it was nearing completion, I decided to take a walk out to see it. Hiking up our steep, unpaved road I spotted a large nut on the ground—the kind of nut that screws onto a bolt. Encrusted with dirt and covered with rust, the nut obviously had been rained on and driven over. Absentmindedly, I picked up a small stick and started scraping out the dirt. Walking up the steep hill slowed my cleaning process, because I had to concentrate on just being able to breathe.

Because of this struggle, I felt a little silly holding onto a rusty nut and considered throwing it into the bushes. But because my father taught me to be litter conscious, I couldn't just toss something that wasn't biodegradable into the bushes. Another side of me reasoned that no one would see a buried nut. Satisfied with this reasoning, I started to throw it aside when I heard a whisper in my heart say, "No, hold onto it." Startled, I asked, "Why?" But there was only silence. Shrugging my shoulders I said, "OK," and started up the hill again.

By the time I reached the top of the driveway I convinced myself that I had been "hearing things," and started to throw the rusty nut aside once again. Just at that moment the Holy Spirit whispered to my heart for the second time. "Look," He said. I looked, and there in the road another nut lay on the ground—identical to the one in my hand. Again the Spirit spoke, "Pick it up." So I picked it up and started to clean it out, just as I had cleaned out the first nut. Before my stick touched the encrusted dirt the Spirit's firm voice spoke, "No, you may not clean this one . . . for it represents Dan, and the other one represents you. Just as you found these nuts far apart from each other, Dan and you are far apart. However, even if you and Dan bond with each other, the two of you will still need to unite with Me. Take these two nuts, show them to Dan, and tell him all that I told you. Dan will tell you what they belong to . . . but remember, what they belong to represents Me."

When entering the house where Dan worked, I sensed my presence didn't exactly bring cheer. Ignoring the dark clouds inside the house, I told Dan how the Lord had spoken a message to me and told me to share it with him. He responded by saying something spiritual like, "Oh really? What did He say to you?" If you've ever experienced a relationship with anyone, you realize it isn't *what* they say, as much as *how* they say it that conveys the true meaning. So what I really heard him say was more like, "Yeah,

right!" I responded quite spiritually as well and said, "Forget it!"—
which really meant, "FORGET IT!"

Somehow we got past each other's stubborn walls, and I told
Dan matter-of-factly what had happened. Still, I couldn't help getting excited remembering the Holy Spirit's words. When my story
was finished, I looked up to see Dan staring wide-eyed and white.
He said softly, "Tell me again—all of it." I complied, trying not to
leave anything out and, at the end of my story, I placed the two
nuts in his hand.

Dan jumped up and ran outside, and when he returned he held
an unusual-looking thing in his hands. He explained that the
"thing" the nuts belonged to was a foundation anchor bolt. Always testing, I asked, "How do you know the nuts belong to this
kind of bolt and not another?" Dan explained, "The nut and the
bolt are made for each other and made from the same material—
iron." He went on to say that it's the anchor bolt with the nut that
secures a house to its foundation. In the days that followed, the
Holy Spirit began to whisper a further teaching in my heart.

A Nut Without a Bolt Is Useless

A nut by itself is useless. To serve its purpose, we must secure it to
a bolt. If we do not unite ourselves with Christ, we are useless and
unable to serve Him. This next Scripture illustrates Jesus as a vine
and the believers as the branches. It shows what we can do with
and without the vine. "I am the Vine; you are the branches. Whoever lives in Me and I in him bears much (abundant) fruit. However, apart from Me [cut off from vital union with Me] you can do
nothing" (John 15:5 AMP).

By uniting with Christ, we can bear fruit. Once united to Christ,
we will walk through a cleansing process of overcoming sin in our
lives that will result in our living fruitful lives.

The Cleansing Process

As we walk through this life trudging through difficulties, we need to submit to God and let Him cleanse us of sin. But overcoming sin can be a real struggle—just as I struggled to climb the hill toward the house that Dan was building. Yet we need to persevere, overcoming temptations to sin, and not giving up—throwing our lives aside, as I considered throwing the nut to the ground. Instead of giving up, thinking we'll never overcome sin, we can anchor our lives upon Jesus by securing ourselves to His foundation. There's no use hiding from the Lord anyway. He knows *exactly* where to find us, and the process needed to cleanse us . . . the same way I found my muddy nut and cleaned it. But remember when I picked up the stick to clean the second nut? The Lord rebuked me, because it isn't my job to clean another's life. It's their job, and God's. To my further amazement, the Lord showed me the process He uses to cleanse us . . .

The foundational anchor bolt had disappeared. In fact, months had passed since Dan had seen the anchor bolt with the two nuts on it. So, when Dan came across them one day while cleaning out his toolbox, I snatched them up and placed them on the mantelpiece above our wood-burning stove. But just when I placed the anchor bolt down, the Spirit whispered into my heart, "Throw them in the fire."

"I don't want them to turn black," I said aloud.

"Trust me," the Lord replied.

"OK," and I placed the anchor bolt—with its two nuts—into the fire.

Later the Lord told me to take it out of the fire, pour oil over both the bolt and the nuts, and scrub them with a wire brush. As I scrubbed away, I saw that they were getting cleaner and that the rust was coming off. The Lord explained that the fire symbolizes the trials of life that expose the things that do not please God and ultimately cause great harm to the believer. When we go through these fiery trials, the Holy Spirit is like the oil, which comforts us, while the Word is like the wire brush that cleanses away the things that can cause us harm. In the same way that rust harms iron by eating away and rotting it, sin harms us by *rotting* our hearts, separating us from God. Jesus takes hold of us and scrubs us through His Word to remove these things that can rot our hearts. Even so, "He will sit as a refiner and a purifier of silver; He will purify the sons of Levi, And purge them as gold and silver, That they may offer to the LORD An offering in righteousness" (Malachi 3:3).

We are like the "sons of Levi" in this Scripture, who go through a purifying process. As the refiner heats up the precious metals, the impurities come to the surface, are exposed and removed— leaving pure gold or silver. The refiner's fire purifies the gold and silver. Jesus is the refiner, who removes the things that cause harm and ultimately separate us from Himself. When we endure fiery trials, the things in our hearts and lives that do not please God can surface. Then, because we see the impurities, we can choose to remove them with the help of Christ.

When researching the refining process of gold and silver, I discovered something that just seemed to jump off the page. One of my resources said that rust doesn't crumble silver, as it does iron. This means we can look forward to a day when the Refiner produces pure silver or gold within us, after which we won't crumble to rust (sin). In other words, sin will no longer have its rotting effect on our lives! I look forward to the day when we face Jesus with a heart of pure gold.

This spiritual refining process helps remove sin, and also helps remove our false perceptions of who God is . . .

False Perceptions

After I took the bolt with the nuts out of the fire, my eyes caught something that caused me to question. "Lord, I understand that the dirt and rust on the nuts represent sin, and that the fire I placed the bolt and nuts into is like the fiery trials we go through. I know You promised to never leave or forsake us, and so You always go through the trials with us. But why does this bolt seem to symbolize that You have rust, too?" Sometimes when I ask the Lord something, I don't get an answer right away. Not so this time! In my heart, I heard the gentle whisper, "That's true—there's rust on the bolt because you have false perceptions of who I am. These false perceptions must go into the fire and be cleansed away so that you may truly know Me."

The Lord showed me two different messages I'd heard as a child that could have caused me to perceive Him in a false way. One message taught that God expresses *only* anger and judgment. The other message taught that God expresses *only* mercy, love, peace, and joy. Through familiarity with the Word, however, we see that God expresses love, peace, anger, judgment, mercy, and many other diverse characteristics. I suddenly realized that we all hold on to false perceptions—some big, and some small. It's through relationship with Jesus and going through trials with Him that we come to know Him and to let go of these false perceptions.

As we let go of false perceptions of who God is, we want to make certain that it's God we are secured to, not false securities. If we aren't truly secured to Christ, we can find a false sense of security in others, and in ourselves—or we may even become insecure.

False Security—*Versus*—Insecurity

A radio minister told his listening audience to test their religion for false doctrines by counting how many people exercised the same faith. He went on to say that if the majority believed a certain way, it was the "right" way. In turn the minority of believers, or those who believed differently, were the ones who believed in false doctrine (heresies or lies).

The Word of God and records of history both refute this. Only Noah and seven other minority-believing people survived The Great Flood, because they were the only righteous people on earth. Over the centuries, the majority killed many prophets of the Old Testament because they didn't want to hear the truth of God. And it was the majority that nailed Jesus to the Cross, and persecuted the early Church.

Of course, to be in a Church that contains a majority of believers does not automatically mean that their beliefs are false or heretical, either! Yet, if the majority is or becomes heretical, it can be very difficult to separate from it. This is because belonging to the majority gives us a false sense of security. Having great numbers of people around us makes us feel certain, safe, and secure. Because we cannot judge truth by the number of people who agree with us, we must always test what we hear. It's only by comparing what we are hearing with the Spirit of Truth and the Word of God that we can clearly discern what is true.

Being in the majority is just one way we can be operating in a false sense of security. Other ways include having things like money, social status, beauty, education, material possessions, or worldly achievements. Lacking some of these can cause people to feel insecure. But believers can also feel insecure if sins past or present keep them feeling continually defeated and unworthy of God's love. When we become insecure, we need to remember that it's not who we are that matters, but Who we know. Apart from Christ, we can't do anything of eternal value anyway!

What truly matters is who or what we secure ourselves to. If we secure ourselves to the solid rock foundation of Christ, we'll find true security. Still, once we find security in the only true foundation, we will need to build our spiritual home with endur-ing building materials, as a doer of the Word and not a hearer only. What is a doer of the Word that is secured to Christ like?

> He is like a man building a house, who dug deep and laid the foundation on the rock. And when the flood arose, the stream beat vehemently against that house, and could not shake it, for it was founded on the rock. (Luke 6:48)

Belonging to the majority of believers or seeking after worldly achievements and advantages to find security is like building your house on muddy earth, without a rock foundation. A house that isn't secured to a solid foundation would be frightening to live in—especially when the winds blow, the rains fall, and the storms of life hit hard. Before the storms of life hit, we need to anchor ourselves on the solid rock foundation of Christ, because only in Him will we find true security. But what materials should we use to build our houses?

> Now if anyone builds on this foundation *with* gold, silver, pre-cious stones, wood, hay, straw, each one's work will become clear; for the Day will declare it, because it will be revealed by fire; and the fire will test each one's work, of what sort it is. (1 Corin-thians 3:12, 13)

We build our spiritual houses with gold, silver, and precious stones. These symbolize the kinds of works that please God, and not works of the flesh—symbolic of wood, hay, and straw. If we secure ourselves to the solid foundation of Christ and build with the right materials, we won't fear the fiery trials because our works will endure through eternity! Here is a beautiful poem about the fiery trials that refine the soul:

Pure Gold

He sat by a fire of sevenfold heat,
*   As He watched by the precious ore,*
And closer He bent with a searching gaze,
*   As He heated it more and more.*
He knew He had ore that could stand the test,
*   And He wanted the finest gold,*
To mould as a crown for the King to wear,
*   Set with gems of price untold.*
So He laid our gold in the burning fire,
*   Tho' we fain would have said to Him, "Nay,"*
And He watched the dross that we had not seen,
*   And it melted and passed away.*
And the gold grew brighter and yet more bright,
*   But our eyes were so dim with tears,*
We saw but the fire—not the Master's hand,
*   And questioned with anxious fears.*
Yet our gold shone out with a richer glow,
*   As it mirrored a Form above,*
That bent o'er the fire, tho' unseen by us,
*   With a look of ineffable love.*
Can we think that it pleases His loving heart,
*   To cause us a moment's pain?*
Ah, no! But He saw through the present Cross
*   The bliss of eternal gain.*
So He waited there with a watchful eye,
*   With a love that is strong and sure,*
And His gold did not suffer a bit more heat,
*   Than was needed to make it pure.*

—Author Unknown

This fiery furnace experience works such an important process in a believer's life that the Lord whispered in my heart another
time in order to teach me again about God's use of severe trials in
our lives. It's clear that the Lord uses these fiery trials to forward
His good plans for us—and to make us a pure and holy people
who please Him. Yet, it's easier to have joy in our trials when we
trust that God indeed has plans for us . . .

"I Have Plans For You"

Abigail woke up and wouldn't go back to sleep. It was three o'clock
in the morning, and she remained wide-awake, batting at her toys:
Big Bird and Cookie Monster. I was batting my eyelids just to stay
awake and reflecting on the personality of Big Bird *versus* the Cookie
Monster. Have you ever noticed that Big Bird is always happy and
joyful? Strange bird. Cookie Monster, by comparison, is needier.
He always says exactly what he wants and, if not heard, he says it
louder. If there's still no response, he shouts at the top of his monster voice, "Me *Want Cookies!*"

I can relate to that.

I concluded that Big Bird has a joyful attitude because of his
ability to soar, whereas the Cookie Monster's attitude is demanding because he continually sinks to greater depths of indulgence.
This caused me to consider my own soaring and sinking. There
have been times in my life when I soared joyfully in spiritual growth,
but my fleshly indulgences pulled me down. After one of these
experiences, I recall an eye-opening conversation with a pastor.

"Pastor George," I said, "I was absolutely soaring spiritually
when the trials came." Attempting to communicate the excruciat-
ing pain of the trial, I continued, "It felt as if someone had cut my
legs off." Now this particular pastor must have felt that same knife
before, because there was a twinkling of understanding in his eyes.
Yet walking away, I questioned myself. "Cut my legs off! What a

horrible thing to say! Why did I say that?!" The Lord began to whisper in my heart.

In this metaphor, He showed me the legs are merely a symbol of fleshy or carnal things that don't please God. Though we certainly need our large legs, a bird doesn't. Just as a bird will find it difficult to fly with large legs, we struggle to soar in spiritual growth when sin weighs us down. Our flesh wants to walk in carnal things, which demand indulgence, but God has a plan to help us, "For I know the plans I have for you," declares the Lord, "plans to prosper you and not to harm you, plans to give you hope and a future" (Jeremiah 29:11 NIV).

The Lord uses a spiritual knife called trials to expose and remove the things in our lives that cause us to sink in sin. We don't need to fear these trials. They're not intended to harm us, but to remove the things that could. Instead of fear, we can have a joyful attitude because God's plan frees us from the heavy pull of sin, enabling us to soar in spiritual growth.

Well . . . maybe I relate to Big Bird after all. Cookie Monster has only one thing on his mind—indulgence. Big Bird in comparison wants to soar. Even so, he has his problems, too. His legs are too large to allow him to fly well, and his wings are too small to keep him up there. Yes, I can relate to that! Like Big Bird's oversized legs, we're all weighed down by sin that needs removing. However, trials do not merely remove sin:

> My brethren, count it all joy when you fall into various trials, knowing that the testing of your faith produces patience. But let patience have *its* perfect work, that you may be perfect and complete, lacking nothing. (James 1:2–4)

Sometimes God uses our trials to cause us, and others watching us, to grow spiritually. Just as Big Bird's wings need to grow so he can remain in joyful flight, we need to grow spiritually so we can soar joyfully—even in the midst of all the various trials that come our way. More than in blessing, it's through these trials that God brings forth His plan in us.

This plan is for us to become "perfect and complete, lacking nothing." Perfect and complete simply means a mature believer. This makes it easier for us to have joy in our trial, or maturing process. Although I still find it difficult to actually rejoice during a trial, I have at least learned to rejoice in the good things that came about because of them. This is not to say that we always understand the reason or results of a trial. But we can trust God throughout them and be encouraged to know that He has good plans for us. This plan isn't to harm us, rather to refine and build us up—like pure gold, mature and lacking in nothing.

My Prayer:

Lord, unite me so firmly upon Your foundation that I become a secure spiritual house. Thank you for loving me so much that You make me the best I can be by removing the things that do not please You. Help me to yield to Your hand while You make me to be like pure gold before You. Amen.

Once we unite with Christ's foundation, we must seek protection from the damages sin can cause us. What are the "defense plans" in the Word that will protect us from sin? How can the armor of God protect us? And what do the seven pieces of our spiritual armor represent . . . ?

TEN
God's Defenses
Against Sin

You are precious
In God's sight.
Your purity is
His delight!

WHAT CAN WE DO TO PREVENT SIN FROM DAMAGING US AND TO NEUTRALIZE its effect on our life?

Poison Oak Oil

Dan and I have many trees on our property so, when money's scarce, we'll sometimes cut up a fallen tree and sell it for firewood. On one such occasion, after climbing up and down a hillside in the woods, loading logs on the pick-up truck, I broke out in a nasty poison oak rash.

If you've never had the "pleasure" of the effect of poison oak on the body, pray that you never do! The rash itches madly and can last for weeks. One special soap seems to help. This soap is rubbed on to cleanse all poisonous oak oil out of the pores of the skin. Sadly for me though, it works best if used *before* a rash breaks out. Too late! So there I sat, feeling downcast, rubbing in the soap and asking God, "Why?" (That really meant, *"Why me?"*) Immediately the Holy Spirit whispered Psalms 119:9 into my heart: "How can a young man cleanse his way? By taking heed according to Your word." Feeling sorry for myself, I didn't expect a real answer from the Lord. Actually, I wasn't expecting an answer at all! But, in the days that followed the Lord gave me this teaching.

Recognizing Good and Evil

Sometime during the late fall months, just before winter, the colorful leaves of the poison oak plant fall off the bushes, turn copper, and are not easily recognized. The logs we had stacked in the truck that afternoon had rolled over these leaves, so when I hoisted a log onto the heap the offending oils transferred invisibly from it to the skin of my arms. The translucent poison of sin affects us much the same way these poison oak leaves did. And just as I would avoid going anywhere near a poison oak plant or leaf again *now*, sins that are obvious to us can be avoided.

But what about the sins that are less obvious, those we may have trouble recognizing? I had no idea there were any poison oak plants or leaves around. My eyes were not trained to recognize the plant without its leaves, nor the colorful, crushed leaves on the ground. (I can now!) How can we train ourselves to recognize sins that are less obvious to us? The Word says that just by *practicing* doing right, the right will become so familiar that we'll soon be able to distinguish it from doing wrong, and recognize good from evil.

I am wiser now and can recognize poison oak in any season, but I've also discovered a defense plan—in addition to keeping away from it—that will always protect me from the poison oak.

Just so, the Spirit whispered into my heart to show me how this plan is much like the defense plans found in the Word of God that can help us to stand strong against sin.

A Defense Plan

When I venture out into the woods again, I plan to wear gloves, a long-sleeved shirt, pants, socks, boots, and other protective clothing. Then to prevent the plant oil from getting into my skin, I'll scrub with the special soap long before a rash breaks out. I may even cut my fingernails so I can't scratch my skin and cause the oil to spread. What similar defense plan can we use against sin? Living in a world full of sin, how do we avoid it—other than leaving this world? God provided us with four defense plans in the Word that will help us to stand strong against sin. These plans are: 1) The Holy Spirit, 2) The Word of God, 3) Fellowship, and 4) Spiritual Armor.

Defense Plan One: The Holy Spirit

Jesus said He would not leave us comfortless, and that He would never leave nor forsake us. So, when Christ rose to be by the Father's side, He sent the Holy Spirit to be our Comforter, Teacher, Director of our paths, and the One that leads us into all truth. Therefore, we can always seek the Holy Spirit for truth, and this truth will keep us from sin (Note: more on the Holy Spirit in Chapter Fourteen).

Defense Plan Two: The Word of God

As noted in Psalms 119:9, we can use God's Word to cleanse our way. Just like my special soap, it works best *before* a rash appears or sin erupts in all its ugliness. Reading and obeying the Word is cleansing and refreshing to our souls. This reminds me of Kevin's dog, Bull's-eye . . .

Eating the Word

Wanting to enjoy the warm summer day, I decided to hold my devotions outside on the deck. Settling into a comfortable lawn chair, I took my Bible in hand, but just as I started to open it someone called me into the house. When I returned, I noticed my opened Bible and, upon further inspection, dampness and chew marks on the lower right corners of its pages. It seems Bull's-eye took "eating the Word" literally! Just so, we should be hungry for the Word, because it is our spiritual food. When we let the words of the Scriptures enter our hearts, they renew our strength. I wonder just how often I've tried to live a victorious life "on empty."

Interestingly, Bulls-eye's name is part of the target used by an archer. The bulls-eye is the center-most mark in the target's circle. If the archer's arrow misses the bulls-eye, it's called a "sin." Even so, if we don't aim for the perfect mark established by God, we may fall into sin. Bulls-eye (the dog) must have thought his name would be changed if he didn't get the Word inside to keep him on target: "Your word I have hidden in my heart, That I might not sin against You" (Psalms 119:11). By hiding the Word in our heart, we can stay within the center-mark and prevent sin—or, in Bulls-eye's case, *avoid getting his named changed* to Sin!

Defense Plan Three: Fellowship

In the fellowship of other believers, we place ourselves in a position to receive the exhortation, encouragement, and restoration through one another. Most believers recognize the need for the Holy Spirit's work in their lives, and see that reading the Word is essential. Yet fellowship is also important, even though we frequently overlook it as a real *need*.

Maybe that's because other believers have hurt us, or maybe we don't realize our human need for fellowship. The Word says not to forsake fellowship or gathering together with believers, especially in the last days. This is because end times prophecies describe difficult times—times when we need each other more than ever. The Lord can certainly use us individually, but we also need to be a working part of the Church. This Scripture shows what happens when we fellowship with other believers: "*As* iron sharpens iron, So a man sharpens the countenance of his friend" (Proverbs 27:17).

We sharpen each other—giving each other "the edge" in all we do. How do we do this? Think of the way a knife is sharpened by a file . . . metal rubbing against metal. Even so, we sharpen each other when we fellowship. This sharpness is referring to our process of becoming mature believers. (Chapter Eleven gives further examples of the benefits of fellowship with other believers to help us stand strong against sin.)

Defense Plan Four: Spiritual Armor

As noted, I plan to wear extra clothes the next time I go into the woods to protect my physical body against poison oak. The Lord whispered into my heart that, much like such protective clothing, putting on the provided "spiritual armor" can protect us from being affected by the sins of this world. And we need to make sure we wear *all* the spiritual armor of God:

> Put on the whole armor of God, that you may be able to stand against the wiles of the devil. For we do not wrestle against flesh and blood, but against principalities, against powers, against the rulers of the darkness of this age, against spiritual hosts of wickedness in heavenly places. Therefore take up the whole armor of God, that you may be able to withstand in the evil day, and having done all, to stand. (Ephesians 6:11–13)

The Seven Pieces of Spiritual Armor:

1. Belt of Truth
2. Breastplate of Righteousness
3. Footgear—Preparation of the Gospel
4. Shield of Faith
5. Helmet of Salvation
6. Sword of the Spirit—Word of God
7. Prayer—Communicating with our King

First Piece of Armor:

Belt of Truth

Ephesians 6:14a: Stand therefore, having girded your waist with truth . . .

Truth in this Scripture is compared to a belt. A belt is a basic unit of the warrior's apparel since it holds up his pants! Without a belt, the pants fall down, exposing a warrior to shame. Just so, the believer is a spiritual warrior. As such, we need to bind the belt of truth securely around ourselves because it keeps us living in God's will. When not wearing our belt of truth, we can fall into false doctrine or sin that will cause us shame.

The belt is also an important part of the warrior's armor since it has a sheath that secures his sword. Without the belt and its adjoining sheath, the warrior could grow weary of carrying his sword. He might grow so weary of holding it that he would drag it along on the ground, causing it to become dull and useless. Similarly, we support our sword, the Word of God, with our belt of truth. As believers, we need this belt of truth to hold on to our sword so we can, "Be diligent to present yourself approved to God, a worker who does not need to be ashamed, rightly dividing the word of truth" (2 Timothy 2:15).

Without truth, we drag our sword along through life. Without truth, we're incapable of rightly "dividing," or using the Word, and our understanding of it becomes dull and useless. As spiritual warriors, we bind truth securely around us, like a belt, in order to prevent personal sin and shame. The belt of truth also enables us to use the Word clearly—avoiding false doctrines.

Second Piece of Armor:

Breastplate of Righteousness

Ephesians 6:14b: . . . having put on the breastplate of righteousness.

In this Scripture, righteousness is compared to a warrior's breastplate. In ancient times, the strong metal breastplate protected the vital organs of the warrior. Without it, an enemy could quickly and easily destroy him. If we fight a battle against our enemy wearing our own righteousness, the enemy could easily destroy us. This is because, apart from Christ, the Bible says, all our righteousness is as filthy rags. But when we accepted Jesus as our Savior, He gave us His righteousness. Christ's righteousness is so pure, Satan cannot accuse us when we stand behind it. Wearing the breastplate, we stand protected from sure spiritual death by Christ's righteousness, not our own. And although we are in the process of becoming more like Christ day by day, we'll never enter heaven by our meager righteousness alone! It's only by faith in Christ and by receiving His righteousness that we enter into salvation, just as this Scripture says: "For He made Him who knew no sin *to be* sin for us, that we might become the righteousness of God in Him" (2 Corinthians 5:21).

So, when Satan comes and accuses you of sin in an attempt to immobilize you—fear not! You can shine your breastplate of righteousness right in his eyes and press forward.

Third Piece of Armor:

Footgear—Preparation of the Gospel

> Ephesians 6:15: and having shod your feet with the preparation
> of the gospel of peace.

Preparing to spread the gospel—the message of salvation
through Jesus—is compared in this Scripture to a warrior putting
on his shoes. A warrior wears shoes to protect his feet from all
types of soil and terrain, enabling him to travel farther and conquer more lands. Without shoes, the warrior would travel slowly
and painfully down his path—the trek eventually causing him so
much pain he quits.

Just as the worldly warrior puts on his shoes to prepare for the
journey to battle, we prepare to spread the gospel. Like choosing
to put on a good pair of shoes, "the preparation of the gospel" is a
good piece of armor that we choose to put on. We prepare by studying the Word so that no matter what questions an unbeliever's heart
contains, we'll be ready to give an answer of our hope. Studying
the Word also helps us to gain a good understanding of the Word,
creating a strong *foothold* against false doctrine and sin. Yet like
the warrior who, without his protective shoes, eventually quit, we
may face similar discouragement if we don't prepare to spread the
gospel. A wise person knows that if the feet hurt, the body is im-
mobilized. Wise believers know that if we aren't prepared to preach,
we'll be frozen and silent.

"Preach the word! Be ready in season *and* out of season" (2 Timothy 4:2a). The word "preach" in this Scripture means to proclaim
the good news of Christ—the gospel. We don't have to be an or-
dained minister or stand behind a pulpit to preach the good news!
The Lord calls each of us to preach it through our daily circumstances. We need to prepare beforehand, so we won't be silent when
opportunity comes to us. With prior preparation, we'll be ready to
travel to numerous battlefronts, joyfully leading many souls to Christ.

Fourth Piece of Armor:
Shield of Faith

> Ephesians 6:16: above all, taking the shield of faith with which
> you will be able to quench all the fiery darts of the wicked one.

Faith in this Scripture is compared to a warrior's shield. The
ancient warrior used his shield as a defense weapon to keep the
enemy's weapon from striking him. If the enemy drew too close to
the warrior, he would use his shield as an offensive weapon—causing his enemy to run. The shield was the most versatile piece of
armor in his wardrobe. The warrior could use this defensive and
offensive weapon to protect himself *and* others. Without his shield,
the warrior was rendered vulnerable to attack. He could fight only
in battles where he was sure to win. If the battle were fierce, he
would have to find a place to hide.

We use our shield of faith much as the warrior does. We can use
it to block the enemy's attacks or, as our faith grows, we can use it to
protect and assist others. By faith we can send the enemy running!
But if we don't use our shield of faith we'll be like the warrior without protection. We'll shy away from being active for Christ, frightened or unwilling to go out and do what the Lord is asking of us.
The Lord has given each of us a measure of faith so, if we've accepted Jesus Christ as our Savior, we all have the shield of faith. But
it's powerless if we don't pick it up, position it, and move forward.

Fifth Piece of Armor:
The Helmet of Salvation

> Ephesians 6:17a: And take the helmet of salvation . . .

Salvation in this Scripture is compared to a warrior's helmet.
The helmet is a classic piece of armor that protected the warrior's

head and mind. The warrior knew that if he didn't protect his head the enemy would seek to destroy him by attacking his mind. A destroyed mind would render his strong body, with its invulnerable armor, entirely useless.

Likewise, when we accepted Jesus into our heart, we received a spiritual helmet: salvation. It's by the cleansing blood of salvation that our mind became renewed. Without salvation, we would possess no other pieces of spiritual armor. Without salvation, we would die not only a physical death, but also a "second death"— the one that will separate unrepented man from God eternally. But if we accepted Jesus as our savior, we were given salvation from eternal death; that is, from eternal separation from God. If you haven't accepted Jesus as your Savior and desire this salvation from spiritual death, you can ask Him into your heart right now (see Chapter Eight for an example of a prayer to receive Christ)! There is no greater protection from sin than Christ's salvation—our "spiritual helmet."

Sixth Piece of Armor:
Sword of the Spirit—Word of God

> Ephesians 6:17:b . . . and the sword of the Spirit, which is the word of God.

The Word of God in this Scripture is compared to a warrior's sword. The warrior used his sword as a weapon to fight the enemy for himself and for the people he loved. Without his sword, the warrior would never enter a battle, since no other part of his armor could defeat an enemy as quickly and powerfully as his sword.

We use the Word much the same as the warrior used his sword. With the Word, we can quickly and powerfully destroy the works of Satan, protecting ourselves and others whom God calls us to defend. Without the Word—the sword of the Spirit—we would be just as fearful of battle as the worldly warrior without his sword. The Lord taught me more about spiritual battles through a snake lying in the road . . .

The Snake That Wouldn't Die

Driving the station wagon out the driveway I spotted a rattlesnake in the middle of the road. Although I dislike snakes, I don't go out of my way trying to destroy them because I realize there *is* a purpose for them—to reduce the number of rodents in the world. However, this particular poisonous snake was too close to the area where my children like to play, so this Mom determined to destroy it.

Moving forward slightly, one of my tires rolled directly over the snake's belly. I immediately pictured a dead snake that could never poison my children. But when I backed up to survey the damages, I watched a very angry snake shake his rattler fiercely as he slithered across the road, then he coiled himself up, ready to strike. Determined to destroy my enemy, I drove toward the snake in an attempt to position the right tire squarely on top of the coil. This maneuver took several tries before I hit the target, then stopped the heavy car. Scooting over to the passenger's seat, I saw the tire parked right on it! Then I slipped back into driving position, gripped the steering wheel, and rocked the tires back and forth until certain of my enemy's fate. Backing up again, I watched in disbelief as the snake, still shaking his rattle fiercely, slithered down the hill.

I sat dumbfounded for a few seconds before speaking out in frustration, "There's *no way* that snake could have lived through that!" The Holy Spirit whispered into my heart.

God showed me that, just as I never intentionally go on snake hunts, believers don't go on demon hunts either—thinking we could easily destroy all demons. But when we do face a demon, God *has* given us the power and authority to run them off, remove them from our territory, and destroy their potentially destructive works. Just as snakes have a purpose, demons have purposes known by God and will not be destroyed until the appointed time! We needn't let them bother us, though. We can take up our powerful "swords of the Spirit" to destroy the work of demons and remove them from our territory. God Himself will destroy them at the appointed time.

Seventh Piece of Armor:

Prayer–Communication with the King

> Ephesians 6:18: . . . praying always with all prayer and supplication in the Spirit, being watchful to this end with all perseverance and supplication for all the saints.

Praying in this verse does not compare to any part of the warrior's armor. The warrior rarely communicated with those above him, because the lowly foot soldier was expected to keep silent and obey orders. Communication with his king couldn't help the warrior fight his opponent. The king couldn't offer personal protection for a warrior because, although the battle was being waged between armies, each warrior fought one on one. Therefore, if he won or lost his battle it was by his own strength alone. No form of communication with the king could offer assistance in the heat of battle. So, though the warrior considered communication from the commander important, he didn't consider it part of his protective armor.

Our line of communication is so vastly powerful that it's a main piece of our armor. That powerful communication is prayer—not to a commanding officer, but to the King Himself—King Jesus. Our King not only directs us in battle, but also actually fights by our side, providing protection. When we fight against sin or wage a spiritual battle, we don't win by our might, but by our King's.

Our King Jesus is not like the kings of this world, uninterested in the lowly foot soldier, expecting silent obedience. How often does Jesus want us to pray? "pray without ceasing, in everything give thanks; for this is the will of God in Christ Jesus for you" (1 Thessalonians 5:17, 18).

To pray without ceasing does not mean we should send up a constant babble to God. It means, rather, that we maintain a habit of including God in every area of our lives. Communication comes naturally when we realize we belong to a loving King who is by our side. Keep the seventh piece of armor, prayer without ceasing, in place and in motion.

When we make use of the seven pieces of armor in our spiritual clothing and implement the other defense plans (Holy Spirit, Word, and fellowship) God's provided to keep us strong from sin–something fantastic happens! We build up immunities in the areas of sin we were once so drawn toward.

Building Immunities

A strange thing has happened since the "poison oak" incident described above: I find I don't develop as bad a rash as I used to before that severe exposure. It appears I've built up immunities against it. However, I'm not so foolish I'd walk through a patch of poison oak bushes! It's the same with sin. As we practice doing right, we learn to recognize good from evil, and by using God's defense plans we become strong in the areas that once drew us to sin. In this newfound strength, we need to be careful not to cause others to stumble and sin . . .

Stumbling Blocks

My friend Sharon was just a little girl when her family went on an outing where poison oak grew in abundance. Being mischievous, she decided to rub poison oak leaves all over her body in hopes that she'd break out in a rash and get to skip school. I can just picture her sitting next to her sister on the way home . . . with a smug look on her face, thinking she was so clever. Sharon got a big disappointment. She not only failed to produce a single rash, but also watched helplessly while her sister swelled so badly she was taken to the hospital!

My heart went out to my mischievous girlfriend because she felt so badly for causing her sister so much pain and, to make matters worse, she had to go to school anyway!

We need to be sensitive, in our newfound strength against sin, to others around us—not causing them to stumble or sin—just as this Scripture tells us: "Therefore let us stop passing judgment on one another. Instead, make up your mind not to put any stumbling block or obstacle in your brother's way" (Romans 14:13 NIV). We don't want to cause anyone to trip and fall into sin!

My Prayer:

Lord, help me to recognize the sins that aren't obvious to me . . . that I might learn to live a pure life for You. Thank you for Your defense plans against sin: 1) Your Holy Spirit, 2) Your Word, 3) Fellowship, and 4) Spiritual Armor. Show me how to use these to help me stand strong against sin. Amen.

🐃   🐃   🐃

If we choose to rebel against God and revisit our sins, we can enter a captivity much like Alcatraz prison. What is the difference between bondage, captivity, and a stronghold? Then how do we remove each? How does God rebuild the weak areas, which draw us toward sin? What materials does He use? Who will help us . . . ?

ELEVEN

No Longer in Alcatraz

The walls once burned and torn down,
Stand firm with tempered mortar.
There is neither affliction nor shame within,
For now you serve the Master.

ARE THE WALLS AROUND US BUILT WITH STONES OF OBEDIENCE OR REBELLION?

The Business Trip

Dan and I went to San Francisco on a business trip, and for a special treat we went to lunch at a beautiful restaurant on the wharf. While we enjoyed each other and the scenery outside the expansive windows, I heard the whispers of the Holy Spirit within my heart. To enjoy the view out the big windows directly in front of me, I had to look beyond a young couple. It was beautiful to watch this couple communicating. Because they were apparently deaf, speech required they give each other their full attention, with constant eye-to-eye contact. To understand each word or thought, they gave rapt attention to gestures, expressions, and their signing hands. The Spirit whispered in my heart about this sign language used by people who are deaf.

This language is a form of communication used by people we sometimes refer to as "disabled." Those who have not experienced being disabled in this way take hearing for granted; *our* conversations are often full of complete misunderstandings. This is usually because our concentration is on ourselves, making it difficult to hear what the other person even said. There are other problems in our conversations, such as pretending to hear, ignoring, frequent interruptions, and infrequent eye contact. Disabled? When I think about this couple, I wonder which of us is truly *disabled*!

Just as people who are deaf have an unusual way of communicating, we believers exhibit an unusual form of communication that the world doesn't understand. When Jesus comes into our hearts, He makes it possible for us to communicate with Him. By living in obedience to God, we won't desire to live in rebellion, but will seek to please Him and to experience His will for our lives. People of this world won't understand us and may even say we're "disabled." If we're living according to the Word, they may even criticize us openly for how we live our lives: "For the message of the Cross is foolishness to those who are perishing, but to us who are being saved it is the power of God" (1 Corinthians 1:18).

But if we choose to live in rebellion to God, we will build walls of rebellion. By erecting these walls of rebellion in an effort to keep God out of our lives, we will find ourselves caught behind the thick walls of a prison of our own making—a prison comparable to Alcatraz.

Alcatraz

Something else seemed to leap out at me when I looked beyond the young couple in the restaurant. *Alcatraz.* I spied the infamous, abandoned prison between them out the large open window. This federal prison had once held dangerous criminals. Situated on a twelve-acre island in San Francisco Bay, the only way on or off of it was by boat. This made escape almost impossible since swirling water and jagged rocks surrounded the island. Today Alcatraz is a tourist attraction. Visitors can buy a ticket for a boat ride out to the island and tour the deserted facility, which once imprisoned hardened criminals for a lifetime.

Today the prison is broken down and out of service, so there are no more locks in use at Alcatraz. Just so, believers are no longer in the bondage of sin. Our bondage to sin has been broken, the doors unlocked, and our souls set free. However, just as tourists visit Alcatraz, we sometimes want to revisit our places of rebellion. When we choose to toy with rebellion in this way as a believer, we risk reentering spiritual captivity. Although bondage and spiritual captivity differ, we can enter both through rebellion. Only salvation's repentance can release us from *bondage*, while *captivity* is broken through repentance and obedience. But what is bondage? And what is a captivity?

Bondage

The Pharaohs of Egypt kept the Israelites as slaves (bondage), but Moses arose to deliver them. Moses is a picture of what Jesus does for us when He saves us from the bondage of sin. Just as the Israelites could not hope to escape without the help of Moses, so it is with us. We are unable to break the bonds of sin without the help of Jesus. Such is the heavy bondage of sin, and God's answer to it is salvation through Jesus. To break a bondage, we simply repent and invite Christ into our hearts. He then enters and frees us from sin's hold.

Captivity

After the Israelites were released from Egypt, they entered the Promised Land and obeyed God (for the most part) for many years. But the Israelites turned away from God and took on the ways of the world. They stopped observing the Sabbath and worshipped idols instead of the one true God. Now our God is patient . . . He waited over four hundred years for His people to turn from their wicked ways and, because they didn't He allowed the Babylonians to take them captive. But the Israelites were not *all* slaves in bondage. The Babylonians actually wanted the captives to learn the ways of Babylon so that they would forget about their homeland and become "Babylonians."

Daniel, a Jewish prophet and godly wise man in Babylon, interceded for the people, praying for their forgiveness and their return to Israel. In response to his prayer, a king came to the throne, whom God caused to make an announcement. The king declared that any Israelite who desired could return from captivity and go to their homeland and rebuild the temple. The king not only sent them, he gave them gold, silver, and materials to help them rebuild!

Believers do not return to the bondage of sin (or at least it is difficult to do so). What we do enter when we rebel against God is *captivity,* resembling the captivity the Israelites experienced in Babylon. To live in rebellion as a believer is to be like the Israelites living in a foreign land like Babylon: They didn't belong there, and neither do we. But sin can "capture" us if we're walking far off from God. At such times, His answer to captivity is to lead us back to repentance and obedience. However, if we allow sin to rule us without repentance, we run the risk of turning captivity into a stronghold. What is a stronghold? And what power must we use to remove one . . . ?

Ridding the House of Pests

A wasp stung my daughter, Desireé, in her bedroom. Investigating, I found the offending wasp in the window and killed it. The next day I found a few more in the same window, and killed them, too. This became a daily procedure. In fact, before I could let the smaller children take a nap I would first perform my daily search for wasps. Although this search began with only a couple of wasps, each day the number would increase. Discovering that they were coming from the ceiling, I reasoned that they couldn't reproduce if I kept destroying them. This seemed to be true, since they appeared to be decreasing in number, and for a few days there were actually *none* found in the windowsill area. But my optimism proved to be false, and they soon returned full force.

I had used an old shoe to *squish* them, and when only a few had appeared in the window it wasn't too difficult. But when numbers increased and then multiplied—it progressed from "not too difficult"—to downright sickening! At those times I tried to remind myself that if I kept destroying them eventually they'd all disappear. However, after killing forty wasps in one session I became sickened enough to seek a better, more permanent way of ridding my home of these pests!

Visiting my friend, Debby, I related the entire wasp problem and asked her advice. She told me that she had fought the same problem when she lived in a mobile home for a while, and that her husband, Eddie, was sure to have a remedy. We approached him, and he gave a quick and sure answer. Eddie said, "Well . . . I guess you've tried poison?" Have you ever searched for your glasses only to have someone calmly tell you they're on your head? I felt about the same way, no—worse! Probably more like looking all over the house for my keys until I finally found them—in my hand! Anyway, I felt pretty silly, so I responded with something like, "Uh . . . (clear throat) no . . . I, uh, hadn't thought of that."

It was like a miracle! No more wasps! No more searching or sickening squishing! I was in heaven! The Lord spoke to my heart in a gentle whisper about these pests. He explained to me that my trying to rid the house of these pests by squishing them one at a time is comparable to trying by sheer will power to get rid of a stubborn sin or stronghold.

Strongholds

The strongholds mentioned in the Old Testament were fortified cities with thick, strong walls to protect the territory they surrounded. These strongholds could protect an ungodly group of people or a godly one. Even so, in the spiritual realm there are walls of rebellion to God that represent "ungodly strongholds," and there are walls of obedience to God that represent "godly strongholds."

Godly strongholds maintain strong hedges of spiritual protection, which is positioned around our souls to thwart the enemy's fiery arrows. How is this done? We become a godly stronghold against the enemy's attacks when we rebuild the broken down areas that draw us to sin. (Rebuilding is taught at the end of this chapter.)

Those "ungodly strongholds" are much like the picture of captivity of the Israelites we saw earlier in this chapter with one great difference: We move into captivity of the Israelites by choosing to live in rebellion to God. But when we choose to *remain* there without repentance, we actually invite the enemy to join us. This is no longer a captivity to sin, but a *stronghold*, with demonic guards at the exit gates who actively hinder us from escaping.

When we try, by sheer willpower, to get rid of these stubborn sins that have progressed into strongholds, the results are just as futile as my method of getting rid of the wasps. Incredibly, the more we try to get rid of the sin, the more it seems to grow. There may even be days when we think we've won the battle against sin, only to discover that it's returned with reinforcements! As time passes, this warfare intensifies and the sin no longer appears simple but difficult and sickening. While trying to remove a stronghold by our own determination sickens us enough, we'll understand plainly that we need a greater Resource than ourselves. Just as I was able to rid the house of pests with a quick, powerful, and obvious resource, we have a quick and powerful Resource too:

> For though we walk (live) in the flesh, we are not carrying on our warfare according to the flesh *and* using mere human weapons. For the weapons of our warfare are not physical [weapons of flesh and blood], but they are mighty before God for the overthrow *and* destruction of strongholds. (2 Corinthians 10:3, 4 AMP)

The Lord showed me how to use the powerful resource He's given us to remove strongholds through a very unfriendly, old dog . . .

An Old Dog

A short time after we moved to a new area I began to experience a feeling that many of the people in our new community faced strongholds to alcoholism. I asked Dan if he felt it and he agreed . . . so we began praying for the people around us.

One sunny day, I decided to take my toddler, Danielle, for a walk in a nearby neighborhood. We drove to a street close by I had never been on. As usual, I methodically pulled the stroller out of the car and we began our walk down the beautiful, forested road. The houses in this area didn't line up in rows like city streets, but were scattered here and there, just as they had naturally developed over the years. As we walked along, I noticed something else scattered here and there—beer cans. Just then the Holy Spirit whispered into my heart, prompting me to pray for the people in every home. Coming near a home, I prayed against the enemy and for the people who lived within to experience salvation in Jesus Christ.

When I came to the end of the street and turned to go back, a large German shepherd positioned himself—ready to attack. Teeth bared and looking like he pumped iron when he wasn't trying to eat people, he stood fifteen feet from me, growling. And there was no way of returning to the car unless we got past him. He had us trapped. Gripping Danielle's hand tightly, I progressively edged forward while praying . . . and looking for a big stick! But every time I got within five feet of the snarling dog, he'd turn and run to take another battle stance. Determined to free us from this intimidating monster, I never stopped walking, praying, and looking for that big stick.

His line-in-battle had changed three times before a woman stepped out of her home and called off the dog. Then she turned to me and said, "Don't be afraid of the dog. He's old and hard of hearing, so he's always trying to make people think he's the boss. But he's not. He knows he has to obey you. If you don't want him bothering you, just tell him to 'get.' Oh, by the way, his name is Budweiser."

She turned to walk back into her home, then stopped and added, "But if you want him to come, just *call him* and he'll come to you!" (There was no chance of that happening!) I laughed all the way back to my car, asking the Lord, "Do I have to meet Bud Light and Miller, too?"

The Holy Spirit whispered into my heart that everything the woman had said about the dog is also true in the spiritual realm. Even my reaction to this old dog represents the actions we need to take in removing a spiritual stronghold.

Removing a Stronghold

Strongholds are removed by repentance of sin, prayer, the Word of God and, when needed—fasting. But don't get frustrated, thinking that to remove a stronghold you must follow a particular set of prescribed rules. Rather, strongholds are removed by relying on the Spirit of God, who will instruct us personally how to do it. We grow more familiar with God's voice as we constantly deepen our relationship through studying and obeying the Word. This enables us to move with the Spirit of God instead of in the strength, knowledge, or experiences of others.

When Satan tries to make us think he can boss us around, we don't need to be afraid of him; we can order him away, and he must obey. Yet spiritual strongholds *can* be frightening. It would have been very frightening for me if I had seen only the German shepherd and not my main source of protection, who is Christ. When we face our spiritual enemy, we should be alert and aware—not fearful. Wisely focusing our eyes on our main source of protection, we walk steadily forward by faith and in prayer, just as I continued to walk, not run, from the dog. The big stick we carry is the Word of God. Satan is like an old dog who knows he must obey those who have the authority. Yet if we are afraid, we can reach out to other believers for help.

Danielle was a little girl when we took this walk. If she had faced the dog alone, she would've been frightened and not known what to do. This is why we keep fellowship with other believers. Like Danielle, there are Christians who are young in their relationship with the Father, who wouldn't know what to do if they faced the enemy alone. But there are wiser and stronger Christians who, because of their faith and relationship with the Lord, can fight the spiritual warfare with us. Although we may turn to one another for help, Jesus is our true Source and the Answer to problems in both the spiritual *and* the physical realms.

Jesus also gave us a perfect example of what our attitude toward demons should be. While we aren't anxious to seek demons out, neither do we live as though they don't exist, nor live in fear of them. Jesus didn't seek out demons. He was just busy about His Father's work. But when a demon crossed Christ's path, He would remove the demon from its territory and destroy its works. This is exactly what we need to do. As God faithfully directs our paths in His will, He gives us His own authority to destroy the work of any demons in that path. When we exercise faith, He'll enable us to defeat the enemy's work by removing his ungodly strongholds.

Whether the Lord removes us from bondage, captivity, or a stronghold of sin, He wants to restore us so that we can stand strong against the enemy. The Lord Jesus wants our spiritual walls restored so that we can withstand all the enemy's arrows and become a godly stronghold for Him. And so He quietly leads us into:

The Restoration Process

We find a clear biblical picture of the restoration process in the Books of Ezra and Nehemiah. The protective walls around the city of Jerusalem were still broken down, even though the temple had been restored by the Israelites who had returned from Babylon. These walls furnished the only protection for the city and the holy temple. But, because sections of the walls remained burned and torn down, leaving large holes and unguarded gates, enemies traveled in and out of Jerusalem whenever they pleased. When Nehemiah, still in Babylon, heard about Jerusalem's suffering and shame because of the broken walls, he prayed for his beloved city's complete restoration. He asked for help, and after a great battle in the spirit, King Artaxerxes sent Nehemiah with troops, supplies, and the authority to rebuild the wall.

Jerusalem's temple, city, and protective walls symbolize our spirit, soul, and the spiritual hedge of protection about us. We, as believers, need the same type of restoration the city of Jerusalem received.

When the Israelites' restored the temple, they also restored their fellowship with God. So it is with us. When we accepted Jesus, our spirits received similar restoration of fellowship with God. But the

Israelites couldn't stop at just restoring the temple, and neither can we. We need to repair the walls of our soul and spirit, just as they restored the walls of Jerusalem, to withstand attack.

The burned and fallen walls of Jerusalem, which allowed enemies to come and go as they pleased, are similar to our spirit's walls when in disrepair. Before we entered the gates of salvation, sin damaged our spiritual walls. This state of decay in our spiritual walls may allow the enemy to bring in temptation wherever sin creates an access. Once inside, the enemy can wreak havoc with our mind, will, and emotions.

Clearly, we need to rebuild the spiritual walls of protection around our spirit and soul (mind, will, and emotions), just as Jerusalem built walls around the city and temple to protect them. The restoration process is the rebuilding of these "cracks" in the wall created by our sin.

Nehemiah is a symbol of the Holy Spirit in our lives. Just as Artaxerxes sent Nehemiah with troops, supplies, and royal authority, our King Jesus sent the Holy Spirit with troops (angels), supplies (Christ's love, mercy, and forgiveness), and authority (God's own). Both Nehemiah and the Holy Spirit have the job of restoring walls of protection to prevent the enemy from attacking God's people anytime he pleases.

Repairing broken areas in our walls makes us overcomers, and enables us to do the work our heavenly Father "whispers" to our hearts. What broken areas prevent you from doing the work of the Father? We need to ask the Lord to reveal His truth to us about the areas sin draws us most easily toward. When in doubt, we might examine ourselves and see—the sins we have the most trouble with are generally the weak holes or areas that need repair.

Do you know who repaired the walls around Jerusalem? Not Nehemiah. He supervised! The people did the work. Each Jewish community repaired the area of the wall closest to their homes.

Naturally the people living by a particular hole or gate were very familiar with it. This means there are people God has placed (or is going to place) in our lives who are familiar (or strong) in an area where we are weak. These people can help us rebuild that area of the wall within our souls. Just as the whole city didn't concentrate on one gate or one hole, the entire Church body doesn't focus on repairing a particular area in our lives. Rather, the Lord uses a great variety of people throughout our lives to build us up.

We can recognize the people God sends by the supplies they use to build with. If the supplies originate from Christ, they will be full of love, mercy, and forgiveness. However, if the supplies originate from self, they will be full of pride, judgment, and unforgiveness. Christ's supplies unite to form a tempered mortar, which creates a durable wall against the enemy. Tempered mortar in ancient times was made of water, straw, and clay. This combination was the "glue" that caused the stones of the wall to bond together. If missing one ingredient, or if the wrong ingredients were mixed into the mortar, the wall was untempered and soon became feeble.

We don't want to build feeble walls. So, we should seek out the people who will build and strengthen us very carefully—those who use Christ's supplies of love, mercy, and forgiveness. They will help us build walls that will endure both the trials of life and the attacks of Satan. Likewise, we should be wary of immature people who might take pleasure in exposing weaknesses, or even cause us further damage, by using their own supplies of pride, judgment, and unforgiveness. Such people will erect an untempered wall, which will eventually crumble and leave a larger hole than before. This Scripture defines what our attitude should be when restoring one another:

Brethren, if a man is overtaken in any trespass, you who *are* spiritual restore such a one in a spirit of gentleness, considering yourself lest you also be tempted. Bear one another's burdens, and so fulfill the law of Christ. (Galatians 6:1, 2)

It's our job to help one another restore the walls of protection, to keep the enemy from bothering God's people. This job is so important to believers that the enemy *will* try to defeat us in the process. We need to be like the Israelites, who carried a weapon in one hand to fight the enemy while rebuilding a wall of protection with the other. The Lord gives us His mighty spiritual weapons of prayer, faith, and the Word because a war is always being waged in the spiritual realm to keep us from this restoration. Obedience to the restoration process makes us a sweet aroma to God . . .

A Smelly Odor—*Versus*—a Sweet Aroma

A friend of mine was very receptive when I shared with her the illustration of Alcatraz and the deaf couple. She spoke of her grandfather—held in isolation at Alcatraz many years prior. During the time he spent in solitary confinement there, he received only onions to eat and water to drink. The purpose was to make him hate even the smell of himself. (Everyone else probably did, too!) When we choose to obey our own selfish lusts and desires by feeding on the rebellion of this world, we get pretty smelly, too, as this Scripture says, "As dead flies give perfume a bad smell, so a little folly outweighs wisdom and honor" (Ecclesiastes 10:1 NIV).

Dead flies in perfume—*yuck!* But when we obediently focus on Him with our whole hearts and minds, our prayers become like a sweet aroma to God. It's much easier to stay out of the folly of sin when restored! But the Lord never forces restoration on us; we always have a free will, which enables us to choose or refuse it. Still, Satan knows all about our free will and seeks to persuade the believer to quit his restoration process by telling us one of his many lies.

The Lie

Satan tries to convince us that being a believer is difficult, and that being obedient to God is disabling. But, remember the deaf couple at the beginning of the story? We may think of them as disabled because they communicate differently than we, but do you remember how well they understood each other? Noises didn't distract them because their full focus and concentration remained on one another. This might have looked difficult to outsiders, but was it? In fact, if we focus on Jesus the way that couple focused on each other, the world will, indeed, think of our lives as difficult and "disabled." Unbelievers often think that the Lord makes our lives difficult, as Satan would have us believe. Rather, Jesus tells us exactly what we can expect:

> Come to Me, all *you* who labor and are heavy laden, and I will give you rest. Take My yoke upon you and learn from Me, for I am gentle and lowly in heart, and you will find rest for your souls. For My yoke *is* easy and My burden is light. (Matthew 11:28–30)

A yoke is a frame with two loops on it for two oxen, usually used in farming to pull a plow or a load. The yoke harnesses the two oxen together. Jesus is saying He's yoked with us. It's not a yoke of bondage or a way of disabling us; it's "easy," and the burden is light. If the burden is heavy, we may be pulling alone, pulling the wrong load, or perhaps being drawn into sin—and that's a heavy load! To prevent being drawn into sin and taking our focus off the Father—we *need* to be an active part of His restoration process. Every believer needs this restoration! Remember, the job is not yours alone, that's why the Scriptures say, "not forsaking the assembling of ourselves together, as *is* the manner of some, but exhorting *one another* and so much more as you see the Day approaching" (Hebrews 10:25).

We need one another to rebuild these areas in our lives where drawn to sin. Even when we want to give up, don't—hold on tight because God our hope is faithful . . .

God, Our Hope, Is Faithful

When Dan and I moved to Northern California, we were totally unprepared for the heaviest snowfall in one hundred years. Actually, we'd grown up in Southern California, and the most we knew about *snow* was from the *playful* (warm) days we'd spent in it! So we were totally unprepared for our initiation to real snow country!

One week after settling in, we awoke to a light, romantic snow. Being of pioneer spirit (which has long since been lost due to fighting with reality), I woke everyone and sent him or her off to work and school. Danielle, then a toddler, and I, seven months pregnant, went back to bed for a cozy nap. An hour or so later we were awakened by the cold and soon discovered the electricity had gone off.

Looking out the window, I received a surprise greeting of snow—three feet deep! Of course I realize this probably isn't very much snow to some people, but it was three feet too much to me! Not knowing how to heat the trailer we were staying in, I decided to try for an escape off the mountain.

Just out the front door our big black Bronco was parked. So I guess I figured with this big bad four-wheel drive I was out-of-there! I figured wrong. With my inexperience in four-wheeling, I didn't realize I was attempting a ridiculous feat. The passenger door was closest, so I proceeded to knock off all the snow. This was no easy task. Although I lacked skill, I excelled in determination.

After much trouble, I cleared off the door panel and I prepared to unlock it. Fumbling with the keys, I at last found the right one. Then, just as I lifted the key to insert it into the keyhole, my addled memory (which had not served me before this) recalled a family incident with this same keyhole, which now rendered it inoperable . . . . A few years earlier, my daughter, Tiffany, had tried to get in the car without the key—figuring a *stick* would serve as well. She soon discovered otherwise, but the stick remained.

Colder, but still determined, I trudged through the deep snow to the driver's side door, resuming the task. But just as I swept off the last bit of snow and raised the key to the lock once more, the tree above me, which I hadn't before noticed, dumped all its snow on top of—you guessed it—my head! I discovered two things: that snow can be very damp but not my determination!

Back inside, I bundled Danielle up and headed out with her in my arms to find a phone. Trudging through the three feet of snow once more, I headed for the manager's home in an effort to reach Dan. When I stepped on the snow-covered front steps, I couldn't locate the step risers. Each time I took a step, I slid back down to the ground. For a good ten minutes, which seemed like hours, I tried to climb those stairs. Finally, I grabbed the railing with one arm and with all my strength pulled us to the top of the porch (The other arm was carrying a toddler, remember?) At first try, the phone lines were dead, but a prayer broke through them and my brother-in-law, John, answered on the other end.

"Dan's on his way to get you, Donna," John reassured me.

Soon I saw my faithful husband blazing through the heavy snow to rescue me. I had mixed feelings that rotated from, "I'm so glad to see you!" to "Why did you bring me to this place?" and, of course . . . "What took you so long?!"

It took two weeks for the electricity to be restored, and much longer for the snow to melt enough to move the Bronco. Driving past the manager's house on our way home, my eyes did a double take when I noticed the snow melted off the "stairs," which had been so difficult to climb. There weren't stairs there at all! It was a ramp! Then I heard the whispers of the Lord speak this Scripture into my heart: "Let us hold fast to the confession of *our* hope without wavering, for He who promised *is* faithful" (Hebrews 10:23).

Just as my weight pulled me down that slippery ramp, the weight of life's trials, temptations, and predicaments pulls us toward defeat. What can we do? The Lord whispered into my heart, explaining.

Even when surrounded by other people, we can feel cold, alone . . . even *stranded*, like I was. I wanted off that mountain—badly— just as we may want out of captivity or strongholds. My determination didn't rescue me, but my determination to get in contact with my faithful husband did comfort me. It helps to know that salvation is on the way. Even so, we can call out to our faithful God and He will give us comfort and help.

Try not to have the attitude I had when I felt like yelling: "Why did you bring me to this place?" and of course: "What took you so long?!" Because, as I discovered, he was already on the way even before I called. So it is with our heavenly Father, who sees our daily predicament. Don't give up on His restoration! Just as I held on tightly to the railing, hold on *tightly* to our hope . . . because our Lord is faithful.

My Prayer:

Lord, some areas in life are so difficult in which to be victorious. It sometimes seems best to just give up. But You can conquer even these areas, Lord. With Your help, I can be victorious in them. Show me the holes in my walls Lord—places where I need to repent. Then lead me to other believers who will love me and help me to build strong, solid walls using Your supplies of love, mercy, and forgiveness. Amen.

❧   ❧   ❧

It takes the light of Jesus to break through the darkness of sin in our lives. When the Lord fills us with His light, He also commissions us to use His light for the good of others. But how do we use that light, and what effect should it have on others? And what happens to the light within us if we fall into a spiritual slumber . . . ?

Twelve
Keep the Candle Burning

You tend the flame.
Your light shines bright.
You stay awake . . .
Through darkest night.

WHAT IS THE LIGHT, AND WHAT HAPPENS IF WE LET IT GO OUT?

The Gift

My friend Debby gave me a beautiful set of lead crystal candleholders. I love beautiful things, but the reality of a large family is that fragile things just seem to get broken—on a regular basis! In spite of this, I didn't want to put both of the candleholders away and miss out on a visible daily reminder of my friend's love. So . . . I put one piece in a well-protected place, but I kept the other out to enjoy—especially on dark winter nights . . .

A Dark Winter Night

Without the convenience of electricity, we've grown quite familiar with candles, relying on them to light our dark nights. One dark winter night, while waiting for Dan to return home . . . with a candle burning brightly in my crystal candleholder . . . with the children fast asleep, I enjoyed a few moments alone. The night seemed to grow long waiting for my sweetheart, and I must have fallen asleep, because I was suddenly awakened by a loud cracking sound. As I lay there foggy-brained, trying to determine exactly what the strange sound was, a picture of shattered crystal flashed through my mind. *Oh, no, my beautiful gift, ruined!* With this thought, I was jolted wide-awake and jumped up to light another candle. To my shame, I found my crystal candleholder just as I imagined. It held the remains of the once-lit candle, but the top of the candleholder was cracked and burned. I was so upset with myself that I just left it there—ugly, broken, and burned. There was no one to blame but myself. If I had stayed awake and tended to the flame, it wouldn't have burned out and caused such an ugly mess.

Not long after this, Debby came to visit. She had rarely been able to come to my home, so I was pleasantly surprised. But, upon re-entering the house after saying good-bye to her, I saw the charred, ugly, and broken candleholder resting just where I'd left it. I felt so embarrassed and ashamed. *Debby must have seen it,* I thought, *and may have imagined that I hadn't cared about her wonderful gift.* The Lord whispered into my heart about the responsibility we carry with the light we bear within us.

Beacons

When we receive Jesus, He places His light within us. "You are the light of the world . . ." the Scripture says. "Let your light so shine before men, that they may see your good works and glorify your Father in heaven" (Matthew 5:14a, 16a). Like spiritual candles, we shine the light of Christ brightly in a dark world. Darkness in God's Word represents sin and the enemy's dark influence on this present world. The candleholder represents the people, talents, giftings, and responsibilities God has entrusted to us. Christ places these beautiful gifts before us so that we may shine our light upon them. But how do we shine our lights?

> You are to live clean, innocent lives as children of God in a dark world full of people who are crooked and stubborn. Shine out among them like beacon lights, holding out to them the Word of Life. (Philippians 2:15b, 16a TLB)

We need to be careful how we live our lives—careful to shine brightly—because we have a very real effect on the "gifts" around us . . .

Bright Beams

One dark night while driving home from church, I noticed that several cars in the opposing traffic lane had only one light on; their other lights appeared to be burned out. Suddenly the Lord drew my attention to the fact that *all* of the cars that were passing by me had their left headlight burned out. *That's strange,* I thought. But I felt the Lord trying to speak to me, so I prayed, "Lord, if you want to teach me something from this, let the next *five* cars shine their headlights in the same manner." Not only did the next five cars shine in the same manner, but all the way home the cars were the same—left headlight burned out, right headlight burning brightly! I began to wonder if this was for real.

Then the Lord whispered into my heart about how we believers need to shine our light in two directions: toward Him, and also in the direction of others. While many of us express our love toward God in His direction (like the cars that shined their right headlights brightly), the left light is dim or even dark. The left headlight represents our outward expression of Christ's love to the people in our lives. It also needs to be burning brightly!

We are the expression of Christ's love on this earth to everyone around us, so we need to beam His love forth radiantly. This reminds me of a beautiful, classic hymn. I could never say it better:

Brightly Beams Our Father's Mercy
by Philip P. Bliss

Brightly beams our Father's mercy
From his lighthouse evermore,
But to us he gives the keeping
Of the lights along the shore.

Chorus: *Let the lower lights be burning!*
Send a gleam across the wave!
Some poor fainting, struggling seaman,
You may rescue, you may save.

Dark the night of sin has settled,
Loud the angry billows roar;
Eager eyes are watching, longing,
For the lights along the shore.

Trim your feeble lamp, my brother;
Some poor sailor, tempest-toss'd,
Trying now to make the harbor,
In the darkness may be lost.

We're the bright beams God uses to shine His light in this dark world. The Lord told me more about our bright lights another time while driving my car, but this time it was during the day . . .

Bright Lights of the Day

Driving along in the rain one day, I turned my lights on so that other drivers could see my car coming. The indicator light, which glows if the bright lights are on, wasn't working. So for a few seconds I was concerned about shining my bright lights in an oncoming driver's eyes. Then I remembered that during the day car lights don't hurt the eyes at all, and this Scripture came to mind: "You are all sons of the light and sons of the day. We do not belong to the night or to the darkness. So then, let us not be like others, who are asleep, but let us be alert and self-controlled" (1 Thessalonians 5:5, 6 NIV).

At this moment the Lord whispered into my heart that because we Christians are children of the day, we are comfortable with light. Children of the darkness are not comfortable with light—especially if it's bright and shines into their hearts! Because this bright light isn't always welcomed, we may want to hide it or make it softer, but this is what Jesus said about it:

> Nor do they light a lamp and put it under a basket, but on a lampstand, and it gives light to all *who* are in the house. Let your light so shine before men, that they may see your good works and glorify your Father in heaven. (Matthew 5:15, 16)

Let your light so shine! But a word of caution: We need to be careful that the light that shines is of the Lord Jesus and not of self. If self generates the light, it will be an obnoxious beam *versus* the beautiful, warm light of Christ. Even though the response we receive from the unsaved may be very similar. While Christ's light offends in the heart of sinners—human light offends with harsh ego. However, the Lord's light contains the power of salvation, while human light is just . . . well . . . obnoxious. If we shine the obnoxious light of self on others, or if we've allowed Christ's light to fade, we can also fall into a spiritual slumber.

Spiritual Slumber

Just as I waited on that dark night for my sweetheart to come home, we believers wait in a dark world for our Jesus to return. We need to tend to our own spirit's fire so that it doesn't go out. If I'd stayed awake that night, my candle's flame wouldn't have gone out (after cracking the crystal around it). Even so, when we fail to stay alert in keeping our spiritual fires burning, we may fall into a "spiritual sleep," the kind that Jesus warns about in this Scripture:

> *It is* like a man going to a far country, who left his house and gave authority to his servants, and to each his work, and commanded the doorkeeper to watch. Watch therefore, for you do not know when the master of the house is coming—in the evening, at midnight, at the crowing of the rooster, or in the morning—lest, coming suddenly, he find you sleeping. And what I say to you, I say to all: Watch! (Mark 13:34–37)

In this parable, we are the servants and Jesus is the Master. Falling into spiritual slumber is neglecting to do the things God has called us to do until He returns. Jesus instructed us to be watchful, because we don't know the day nor the hour when He will return. Until that day, Jesus continually provides us with meaningful work and leads us toward the responsibilities He entrusts to our care. If we fall asleep spiritually, we can cause damage to those for whom we are responsible, just as I damaged my precious candleholder when I fell asleep. By contrast, when we stay alert and keep watch, the light of Jesus within us will shine so brightly that we won't be stumbling in darkness. The Light will clearly show us—and show others—the good way.

No Stumbling in Darkness

I've become good at walking through our dark house at night, as long as everything is where it's supposed to be—like the candles and matches! In this Scripture, Jesus promises to give us living light if we'll follow Him: "I am the Light of the world. So if you follow me, you won't be stumbling through the darkness, for living light will flood your path" (John 8:12b TLB).

I'm so glad Jesus doesn't send us out into a dark world to find our way by stumbling through the darkness. Because I live in a dark house without electricity, where I endlessly stumble, I have a particular fondness of this next Scripture, which refers to our eternal dwelling place in heaven: "And there shall be no night there; and they need no candle, neither light of the sun; for the Lord God giveth them light: and they shall reign for ever and ever" (Revelation 22:5 KJV). Imagine that . . . no darkness throughout eternity—and I can throw all my messy wax candles away! Praise the Lord!

My Prayer:

"THE LORD is my light and my salvation; Whom shall I fear? The Lord is the strength of my life; Of whom shall I be afraid?" (Psalm 27:1) Amen.

❧   ❧   ❧

By performing all the duties of a New Testament priest unto God, we become a shining light for Him in this world. But when we neglect to fulfill our duties, we can fall into a spiritual slumber. What are the duties of a believer / priest today? And how do they compare to the duties of a priest of the Old Testament . . . ?

THIRTEEN

Our Priestly Duties

As a priest we offer up
The sacrifice of praise.
We seek Him, love Him, and adore Him
Throughout all our days.

UNDERSTANDING THE TEMPLE AND THE PRIESTLY DUTIES OF THE OLD TESTAment times helps us to understand our duties as believers in New Testament times. What are these duties?

The Temple and the Separations

God designed the temple with six different areas. Starting at ground level outside the temple and moving inward to the most central room of the temple, we discover each area rose to a higher level than the last. With each area, there was a separation to remove the clean from the unclean. Fewer and fewer people were permitted to walk into the inner rooms of the temple, until only one person remained—the high priest.

The progressive "separations" began by removing the Jews from the Gentiles; then the men from the women; next, the priests from the laymen; and, finally, the singular high priest from all the Levite priests. The last, most inner compartment consisted of two areas in one room, divided by a thick, heavy, linen cloth or "veil." These were: the outer room, called the Holy Place, and the innermost room of the temple, called the Holy of Holies.

The Holy of Holies

God accepted the sacrifice for man's sin only in the Holy of Holies or inner room, showing that God considered *it* the most sacred area of the temple. Once a year, on the Day of Atonement, the high priest entered the Holy of Holies to offer the annual sacrifice to cover the sins of the people. To enter the Holy of Holies was to go beyond the veil, that final partition that separated the clean from the unclean.

Ceremonial cleansings and sacrifices were required for both the priest and the Israelites before the high priest could gain admittance into the Holy of Holies. And if the high priest failed any of the cleansing requirements, he'd die instantly when he entered the presence of God (see Lev. 16), and be pulled out of the room by a rope tied around his ankle! In this impersonal way, the people fellowshipped with God, until He revealed His greater plan—held from the beginning of time—to give us "The Way" to fellowship with Him more intimately.

The Way

Death didn't happen because God is unmerciful. God is so very pure and holy that we cannot exist in His presence with the sin we have in our hearts—it would kill us! Adam's original sin had stained us and separated us from our Father, and there seemed no just way to bridge the gap between that sin and His holiness. But God, in

His great mercy, sought to restore us to Himself by sending Jesus to be "The Way." He became "The Way" for us to gain entry to the very Holy of Holies and to even closer fellowship with God. Jesus said: "I am the way, the truth, and the life. No one comes to the Father except through Me" (John 14:6).

When Jesus died on the Cross at Calvary, the thick, heavy veil at the entrance to the Holy of Holies supernaturally tore from top to bottom, from heaven to earth, from God to ourselves. Jesus had become our High Priest and offered His own life and blood on the altar to atone (or pay) for the sins of the world. And because God forgives our sins when we acknowledge and personally accept His sacrifice, we may then ourselves enter the Holy of Holies to enjoy fellowship with God. We no longer need separations that keep us from God. In fact, there is no more separation!

No More Separation

When Jesus died, He did away with the separations in the temple:

Between Jew and Gentile:

For there is no difference between Jew and Gentile—the same Lord is Lord of all and richly blesses all who call on him (Romans 10:12 NIV).

Between man and woman:

There is neither Jew nor Greek, slave nor free, male nor female, for you are all one in Christ Jesus (Galatians 3:28 NIV).

Between priest and layman:

To Him who loved us and washed us from our sins in His own blood, and has made us kings and priests to His God and Father (Revelation 1:5b, 6a).

New Testament Temple and New Testament Priests

Today we no longer require a temple made from earthly materials by the hands of men. When we accept Christ's sacrifice for our sins, He enters our hearts and dwells with us, making our physical bodies the temple of God. He not only made us the temple; He also made us priests, as this Scripture tells us: "But you *are* a chosen generation, a royal priesthood, a holy nation, His own special people, that you may proclaim the praises of Him who called you out of darkness into His marvelous light" (1 Peter 2:9).

Now we need to know what our duties are as ministering priests before God.

FIRST PRIESTLY DUTIES: VERTICAL MINISTRY

Our first duty to be performed in the role of priest is ministry to God. The offerings and sacrifices we now place before God are no longer the blood of bulls and lambs, since Jesus provided the only perfect sacrifice for sin, Himself—fulfilling the law's requirement. The sacrifices we offer now are spiritual and pertain to worship and fellowship with God, as we see in this Scripture: "you also, as living stones, are being built up a spiritual house, a holy priesthood, to offer up spiritual sacrifices acceptable to God through Jesus Christ" (1 Peter 2:5).

How do we minister these spiritual sacrifices? When reading 2 Kings, the Lord whispered into my heart showing me how we minister these spiritual sacrifices to Him as His priest. . .

The Widow and the Oil

In the fourth chapter of 2 Kings, there's a fascinating story about a widow and her two sons. Now the widow's husband had been a prophet and had known Elisha, one of the greatest prophets of that day. So, when a creditor said he was on his way to take the widow's two sons as slaves in payment for the debt she owed, the desperate widow sought out Elisha for help. When he asked her if she owned anything of value in her house, the widow said no, but told him of her one remaining item of value—a cruse of oil. The great prophet advised the widow to go to her neighbors and borrow empty jars . . . then to take her two sons inside the house, close the door behind them, and fill each borrowed jar with a bit of the oil. Obediently, she did so, and God responded with a miracle. She discovered enough oil in the borrowed jars to cover the debt and then some—enough for her family to live on!

The widow and her sons did what we do in our first priestly duty to God: vertical ministry—God gives to us, we return His gift by giving to God. By imitating the widow, we can shut the door against the enemy through prayer, preventing him from robbing us. Notice how often God requires us to take what we have in hand, no matter how little, broken, or worn out. Then God sends His refreshing. When we present what we have to God, He fills His vessels with His oil. The Word often refers to oil as a symbol of the Holy Spirit. In His fullness, we're able to fulfill all the duties of priests. Let's see some of the ways we minister to God as His priests:

Priestly Duties: To God

1. A LIVING SACRIFICE—Our Bodies—Romans 12:1

2. A BROKEN AND CONTRITE HEART—Psalms 51:17

3. OUR PRAYERS—Psalms 141:2

4. OUR SACRIFICE OF PRAISE—Hebrews 13:15

5. THANK OFFERINGS—Psalms 116:17 / Ephesians 5:20

6. LIFTING UP OF HANDS IN WORSHIP—Psalms 134:1–3 /
   1 Timothy 2:8

7. OFFERINGS OF RIGHTEOUSNESS—Psalms 4:5 / Malachi 3:3, 4

8. SERVICE TO GOD—Exodus 28:1 / Hebrews 12:28

These *spiritual* sacrifices, mentioned throughout the Bible, demonstrate what God desires most: fellowship with man through acts of priestly worship "in spirit and truth". Unlike the Old Testament sacrifices God commanded we perform, we give New Testament spiritual sacrifices out of a heartfelt desire to please God. Rather than from a self-righteous or fearful heart, we willingly offer to our Lord what He shows us will please Him most.

However, if we know what God desires from us and we refuse to offer it to Him . . . we can lose our sense of closeness to God, as noted, falling into a spiritual slumber. Yet when we offer up the sacrifices that please God, He rewards in many ways. Most importantly, we develop a deeper relationship with God Himself, which is its own reward.

This deepening relationship develops when we do as the widow did: shut the door against the enemy and pray. Continuing in prayer, we bring other people to God, just as the widow brought her neighbors' vessels—then God sends the refreshing oil to meet all our needs. This moves us on to the second part of our duty as priests . . .

SECOND PRIESTLY DUTIES: OUTWARD MINISTRY

Bringing others to Christ is our second priestly duty or outward ministry, which is person to person. Ministering to our brothers and sisters in Christ and to the lost in the world is a very important duty of the believer / priest. Our hearts and hands—once raised up to heaven in repentance, worship, praise, service, and thanksgiving—can now reach out to minister love, comfort, exhortation, the preaching of the Gospel, care of the poor, and other forms of outward ministry. Let's look at some of the ways we minister to others as His priests:

Priestly Duties: To Others

1. LOVE AND COMFORT—Matthew 5:43–48 / 1 Corinthians 13

2. PREACHING AND ENCOURAGEMENT—Mark 16:15 / 2 Timothy 4:2

3. PRAYER AND INTERCESSION—Ephesians 6:18 / 1 Timothy 2:1–4

4. PRESERVATION OF KNOWLEDGE—Hosea 4:6 / Malachi 2:7

5. CARE FOR THE POOR—James 1:27

6. BEARING ANOTHER'S BURDEN—Galatians 6:1–5

7. LAYING ON OF HANDS FOR:
   a. *Consecration or Ordination for Service:* Acts 6:5, 6 / 1 Timothy 4:14
   b. *Blessing:* Mark 10:13–16
   c. *Healing:* Mark 16:15–18 / Acts 28:8
   d. *Holy Spirit:* Acts 19:2–6

8. SERVICE TO OTHERS—Galatians 5:13

To be able to perform *both* of our priestly duties we need to have a humble heart that seeks to please God. We don't please God when we're questioning His will or ways. This doesn't mean we can't be curious or express our desire for further understanding. Rather, such questioning refers to our refusal to obey because we mistrust His desires or find them undesirable. Sometimes we may question God's will because we feel uncomfortable with it, as Naaman did . . .

Questioning God's Will or Ways

Again while reading in 2 Kings, the Lord whispered to me about questioning His will or His way of doing things. The story tells of a man called Naaman, a commander in the army of the King of Aram. He was a valiant soldier, yet also suffered from leprosy. Naaman accepted the advice of his servant to travel to Israel and

seek healing for his incurable disease by consulting with the prophet
Elisha. But Elisha didn't speak to Naaman personally. He sent his
messenger to tell Naaman to dip seven times in the Jordan River,
and Naaman was angry! I must admit I can relate to Naaman–
sometimes I have this attitude, too. Naaman complained to the
men with him:

> Indeed, I said to myself, "He will surely come out *to me*, and
> stand and call on the name of the Lord his God, and wave his
> hand over the place, and heal the leprosy." *Are* not . . .the rivers
> of Damascus, better than all the waters of Israel? Could I not
> wash in them and be clean? . . . (2 Kings 5:11, 12)

Because Naaman had his own idea how Elisha should heal his
leprosy, he questioned the prophet's way. Naaman's unbending pride
caused him to leave Elisha's house in a rage. It was a good thing
that some of his men talked him out of questioning. They said
something like this: "If that prophet had told you to do something
great you would've done it, Naaman. So you should do this—it's
so easy!" Naaman reconsidered and dipped seven times in the Jordan River, received his healing, and then met the prophet Elisha!

Doesn't that sound familiar? It does to me. If we do as Naaman
did and walk away from the desires of God by questioning His
will or ways, we only hinder our relationship with Him. The reason we don't always understand God is because of what God says
of Himself:

> "For My thoughts *are* not your thoughts, Nor *are* your ways My
> ways," says the Lord. "For *as* the heavens are higher than the
> earth, So are My ways higher than your ways, And My thoughts
> than your thoughts." (Isaiah 55:8, 9)

God doesn't desire that we become mindless robots; rather, people who trust in Him. And He gives us a clear promise if we choose to trust: "Trust in the Lord with all your heart, And lean not on your own understanding; In all your ways acknowledge Him, And He shall direct your paths" (Proverbs 3:5, 6).

How can we, as priests of God, keep from questioning His will or ways? By coming to God just as Jesus said to in this Scripture: "Assuredly, I say unto you, whoever does not receive the kingdom of God as a little child will by no means enter it" (Mark 10:15).

Simple faith—the kind a little child possesses—is what enables us to receive the kingdom and to walk in His will. This reminds me of a scene I've witnessed numerous times: a child standing on a large rock, stuck. When his father stretches out strong arms, calling to the child to jump, he doesn't analyze Dad's strength, capability, or character. The child doesn't think of such things—only of his or her love for Daddy. In all the years I've witnessed this scene, I've never yet seen a child refuse Dad's call. Rather, the child squeals with joy while leaping eagerly into Dad's safe, loving arms. Like these little children, God desires for us to come to Him with our hearts fully trusting, putting aside prideful questioning of His will or ways. When we put aside the pride and self-will of questioning, we can then truly offer the sacrifice of praise . . .

The Sacrifice of Praise

While teaching my teenagers why we lift our hands in worship, I explained to them that people don't raise their hands just because other people do. My teenage daughter, Tiffany, responded with a profound statement, "Who would?!" After we all laughed, I said, "That's why it's called a *sacrifice* of praise!" What we sacrifice to obey God is our pride and self-will. It's a joy to see my children obey God in heartfelt desire to be obedient in giving the spiritual sacrifices in worship as priests to God.

By being obedient, we become like Naaman. Even though he was angry because he didn't like the prophet's instructions, he received his wise counsel as from God and decided to obey. And what was his reward? He was cleansed, healed, and introduced to the prophet! By being obedient to all of God's instructions, and not questioning His will or ways, we can fulfill all of our duties as priests. Then we will enjoy fellowship with our Prophet and Lord, Jesus!

My Prayer:

Lord, "Let my prayer be set forth before thee *as* incense; *and* the lifting up of my hands *as* the evening sacrifice" (Psalm 141:2 KJV). Give me the spiritual oil I need to be a priest toward You and toward others. Amen.

The priest, filled with the oil of the Holy Spirit, is able to minister upwards to God, then outwards toward others. What do we need to do to receive an infilling of spiritual oil? How do we surrender our lives to receive it? And what are the ways in which we pour out this oil to others . . . ?

FOURTEEN
Total Surrender

I surrender all to You,
I'm filled with power from on high.
Let me be a witness,
To draw all men to Thee.

WHAT DO WE NEED TO DO TO SURRENDER?

The Swimming Hole

One warm summer day we went on a family outing to a place we always refer to as "The Swimming Hole." It's located in the foothills of the California Sierras, on the South Fork of the American River. The natural beauty of this area is so intense it is much like an exotic picture from a distant land. At our swimming hole, there's a shallow pool where crystal clear water moves gently over the sandy riverbed. Because of its tranquility, this is where our small children generally play. Moving up the river, the water level changes from ankle, to waist, to shoulder-deep. Then the water begins to move more rapidly. And as the river deepens, so does its color. Up the river again, close to the shallow pools, is a favorite place for the older children—about ten feet deep and fifteen feet across, making it the deepest and darkest pool. What makes this pool so beautiful and fun for kids is the waterfall flowing into it as it cascades down the river to the shallower sections.

My teens liked to take turns climbing to the top of the waterfall to perch themselves on the edge—letting their legs dangle over the rocks. Lifting their faces toward the sun, they would close their eyes, soaking in its warm rays. I'd watch as the cool, moving swirls of water softly surrounded my child before it rushed to the edge and splashed over into the pool below. When the swimmer had gathered enough courage, he'd join the flowing water's current by sliding off into the waterfall—plunging into that deep pool of water below. In just seconds, a head would pop up and the hills would echo with the peals of laughter.

This looked like so much fun that I ventured to do the same. I sat on the edge, legs dangling over, warm sun on my face, cool water swirling, rushing, and then the splashing . . . but, something was missing: the courage to plunge over the edge! Ahh, but no one can sit on the edge of decision for long; even "no decision" is a decision, right? And my teenager, Desiree', was making her way up to the waterfall with a twinkle in her eye, revealing her intent to help me with mine! After convincing her that pushing me in would not have good consequences for her, we sat. Finally I surrendered. From the look on her face you would have thought I'd offered her an all-expense-paid trip to the mall! In I went. The cool refreshing water felt great.

Swimming to the other end of the pool, I discovered my wristwatch was missing! The search began, yet finding it seemed hopeless. As Dan searched the area under the waterfall, I swam to a big rock to catch my breath. While sitting there, an impression overwhelmed me that the watch lay along the base of the rock I now occupied. Immediately I called for Dan to come over and look there for it, but he didn't hear me.

Actually, there was no logical reason for the watch to settle in that particular spot. I even cupped my hands over the water in an effort to see the bottom of the pool. *Useless*—too dark. Yet instead of the feeling diminishing, it increased. I not only felt strongly that the watch was down there, but that it lay between two small rocks at the base of the large one I now rested upon. I couldn't shake the longing for my watch, so I considered diving down myself to search for it. Remembering that water stings my eyes, however, I decided to be patient and wait for Dan. Soon enough Dan swam over stating that the watch couldn't be found and it was time to go home.

"Dan," I said, "I think I see my watch down there between two small rocks. Would you go down there and get it for me?"

Dan looked at the water where I'd pointed, then at me in disbelief and responded, "Donna, you can't possibly see two rocks, much less your watch. It's too dark!"

I felt a little foolish. After all, I'd already tried unsuccessfully to spot my watch. Yet the feeling that it rested in that exact location persisted.

"I know you're right, Dan" I said, "but I really think it's down there. Would you dive down just *once* for me?"

Down he went and, within seconds, surfaced with his hand emerging first to reveal his treasure—my watch! Then came his smiling face. "So, what's the Lord telling you now?!" He asked.

Laughing with joy in the knowledge that He *was* going to show me something, I answered, "I don't know, but whatever it is it's *wonderful!*" And it is! The Holy Spirit began whispering to my heart, teaching me about something truly wonderful.

The Baptism of the Holy Spirit

The level of the water in these pools represents the level of depth or amount we've surrendered our lives to God. Many times we're apprehensive in surrendering to the Baptism of the Holy Spirit because it seems easier to remain in the shallow water, where it feels safe. The gently flowing clear water, the soft sand—this is a comfortable place, where we can rely on our own five senses to keep our lives in control. On the other hand, it appears frightening to give up "our" control by total submersion in the deep, dark waters. But to be baptized, we must surrender totally to the Spirit because we cannot move ahead by what we see—only by trusting the Spirit's direction.

How high is the water level in your life? Is it around your ankles, waist, or shoulders? Or are you still on the shoreline, testing the water with your toes? Let's challenge each other to surrender completely, giving God full control of our lives . . . then we'll be fully immersed in Him.

Remember how I allowed Desiree' to push me in the water? She didn't do it by force—she waited, with joyful anticipation, for me to surrender. So it is with Jesus. He doesn't force His baptism upon us. He waits for us to surrender our will to His best. When we let Jesus baptize us with His Holy Spirit, we can experience a joy much like what I experienced when I popped up out of the cool, refreshing water. We find great joy in total surrender to God!

The water level coming up over my head is a symbol of surrendering all, even fleshly or natural reasoning, to receive spiritual understanding. The darkness of the pool's water is a symbol of the inability of our natural mind to understand or accept what comes from the Spirit of God. In surrender, we become truly wise—not in other people's eyes, but in God's eyes. When we are willing to surrender all to the Lord, we become totally immersed in Him. With the Holy Spirit's fullness, we receive spiritual understanding.

But how do we *see* spiritual things? "For now we see in a mirror, dimly, but then face to face. Now I know in part, but then I shall know just as I also am known" (1 Corinthians 13:12).

Mirrors in ancient times were foggy and dull—not clear like the mirrors we have today. The word *then* in the verse above refers to when we are with Jesus . . . *then* we will have all knowledge and understanding and we'll see all things clearly because we'll see Jesus face to face. But for now, in this world, we see spiritual things only dimly. As the verse says, it's like looking in an old fashioned mirror; what we do see, we see dimly, by faith. The Spirit showed me my watch, but I could only see it dimly. I didn't see it with my physical eyes, but with *a knowing* revealed by the Holy Spirit, who was whispering into my heart. He gave the knowledge. Then, by asking in faith, I received it.

We accept salvation through the meek faith of a child, and so it is with receiving the Baptism of the Holy Spirit and His gifts. As I rested on the large rock, representing Jesus, I desired my watch. Just as I desired my watch, then asked for it and received it, when we desire and ask for the Baptism and the spiritual gifts—we will receive. We won't need to search anxiously, just as I didn't have to search for my watch. Similar to the way in which I waited on the big rock for Dan to bring me my watch, we may need to wait on receiving spiritual gifts. This waiting isn't with the attitude, "If it's God's will, I'll receive." Rather, this waiting is similar to the way I waited on the rock, anticipating and expecting to receive my desire. The disciples waited like this after Christ's death in the Upper Room. They were waiting for the promised Holy Spirit and His gifts.

One of the methods mentioned in the Word for believers to receive the Baptism is through the laying on of hands by others, as symbolized by the two rocks at the base of the large one. People can lay hands on us and pray for us to receive the Baptism of the Holy Spirit and His gifts. One of the two small rocks at the base of the large one represents key spiritual leaders in our lives, such as a pastor. The other represents our sisters and brothers in the Lord. Although the laying on of hands isn't a requirement, other people can encourage our faith in receiving the Baptism and spiritual gifts.

The Gifts of the Spirit

My friend Patty heard this teaching and said, "Donna, I liked the part about the necklace!"

"The necklace?" I asked, "What do you mean, what necklace?"

"You know, the part where Dan found the necklace, or was it a ring? Anyway, I think you should write more about the gifts."

"Oh," was all I could say because right away I knew the Holy Spirit had whispered into my friend's heart to say this, and to show me exactly *how* to teach more about the gifts.

It's interesting that the Lord used my watch, and not a ring or a necklace, as a symbol to me of the spiritual gifts. The gifts of the Holy Spirit aren't badges or ornaments to make us look good or appear as super-spiritual saints. Spiritual gifts have a purpose and a function, just as a watch does.

These gifts are for the equipping of Christians or for edifying and encouraging the Church, giving us the power to be victorious witnesses, as well as overcomers. The gifts are also a sign to non-believers, helping to spread the gospel and power of God. These are the spiritual gifts of the Holy Spirit, not the natural or learned talents we all have, though the world would be a dull place without those talents! The gifts of the Holy Spirit do not point to our abilities, as natural gifts do. They point directly to God—to His power and the power of His love for us.

The gifts of the Holy Spirit are: the word of wisdom, the word of knowledge, the gift of faith, the gift of healing, the working of miracles, prophecy, the gift of discernment of spirits, speaking in a known or unknown language, and interpretation of tongues. Isn't this a fantastic list of gifts? And yet the least of these gifts is still the most misunderstood.

The Misunderstood Gift

The most misunderstood gift is the gift of speaking in tongues, or the *unknown* language. It's called an unknown language because it's not a learned language. This is a language of the Spirit, used to communicate with God—a speaking of words that surpasses our natural understanding. Speaking in tongues, as it is called, will edify (or build up) only the person speaking. This is the reason it's called the *least* of the gifts (not because tongues are unimportant or unnecessary). Rather, because this gift is for the individual and is not a gift that gives edification, or *instruction*, to the multitudes. "He who speaks in a tongue edifies himself, but he who prophesies edifies the church" (1 Corinthians 14:4).

When we pray with tongues, we're seeking the spiritual refreshment we need from God and receiving inward power from the Holy Spirit. As we receive this *edification* from the Holy Spirit, we can minister outwardly as priests to others through additional gifts of the Spirit, like love, faith, and intercession. But what happens when we don't use our gifts or, worse, discard them?

Neglected or Discarded Gifts

Taking Tiffany to school one morning, I noticed she was wearing her watch. So I asked her what time it was. Even though she never looked at her watch, she answered,

"I don't know."

"But, you're wearing your watch," I said.

She looked down at her watch and laughed, "Oh . . . I know, but it doesn't work."

Baffled, I asked, "Tiffany, why would you wear a watch that isn't working?"

She smiled and gave me an obvious teenage answer, "Because it looks good!"

The next morning when driving her to school, I noticed the watch was missing. I asked her why. She said, "It got annoying. Everyone kept asking me what time it was, and then I'd have to explain why I didn't know."

The Holy Spirit began whispering into my heart telling me about some Christians who were baptized in the Holy Spirit and who had received gifts. But for reasons ranging from neglect, compromise, or hurt by other Christians, they had stopped using their gifts. The gifts had become merely a badge or an ornament of the past—a memory—instead of a useful tool for the present. After a time these Christians may deny they ever received gifts, and may even deny the powerful work of the Holy Spirit. Just as Tiffany grew tired of wearing her watch because it no longer served any use, these Christians have grown weary because they didn't maintain their gifts actively.

Instead of my daughter throwing her watch away, I suggested we replace the battery and have it working as good as new! If you have neglected your gifts, as my daughter did her watch, then stir up the gifts given to you and ask the Spirit to recharge you! And then do as these two Scriptures say:

1. Do not neglect the gift that is in you (1 Timothy 4:14a).

2. Therefore I remind you to stir up the gift of God which is in you through the laying on of my hands (2 Timothy 1:6).

Because we're uncomfortable with the Baptism of the Spirit, we may seek a "safe, comfortable" doctrine that actually grieves the Holy Spirit and become like the Laodicean Church. It's sad to realize that the people in the Laodicean Church are *Christians*. So, what Jesus is saying in these Scriptures is for us to hear, also—repenting where we need to.

The Laodicean Church

In the book of Revelation, Chapter Two, Jesus prophesies to John the Apostle. In the fourteenth verse, Jesus speaks to the Laodicean Church:

> I know your deeds, that you are neither cold nor hot. I wish you were either one or the other! So, because you are lukewarm—neither hot nor cold—I am about to spit you out of my mouth. You say, "I am rich; I have acquired wealth and do not need a thing." But you do not realize that you are wretched, pitiful, poor, blind and naked. I counsel you to buy from me gold refined in the fire, so you can become rich; and white clothes to wear, so you can cover your shameful nakedness; and salve to put on your eyes, so you can see. Those whom I love I rebuke and discipline. So be earnest, and repent. (Revelation 3:15–19 NIV)

The first charge against the Church is that it's not cold or hot, but lukewarm. Lukewarm is a comfortable temperature. It doesn't move us in any direction. It's a place of complacency. What makes this complacency so severe is the haughty attitude that sees no further need for God. These are the ones standing on the shoreline in our story, saying they're rich and have no need for anything (or anyone). I can almost hear myself saying, "Oh, this isn't me! I *know* I need God!" But the inner whisper responds, "How much? Are you up to your ankles, your waist, your shoulders—or are you in total surrender?"

The problem in the Laodicean Church goes deep. Jesus says we often don't even realize that we're wretched, pitiful, poor, blind, and naked. In spite of this, we're not without hope. Jesus desires for us to receive His spiritual riches so that we will be *truly* rich. He wants us to be clothed in His robes of righteousness to cover our nakedness (sin) so we'll carry no painful shame. He wants us to choose to have our eyes anointed so we'll see clearly. You see, we bear responsibility for *desiring* to see truth. We need to be as the Bereans in the book of Acts, who didn't just accept Paul's preaching. This is what they did to search out truth, "they received the word with all readiness, and searched the Scriptures daily *to find out* whether these things were so" (Acts 17:11b).

We should respond this way, too, when we want to know truth; search it out in the Scriptures and listen to the Holy Spirit. Let's trust God with our whole hearts and ask the Holy Spirit to anoint our eyes so we can see truth. Then ask the Holy Spirit to help us to surrender all—not just to the ankles, waist, or shoulders, but *all*—allowing Jesus to baptize us with the Holy Spirit!

My Prayer:

Lord, You are my Baptizer. I surrender all to You. Immerse me in Your Spirit. Empower me with Your gifts—not that I would *look* spiritual, but so that I will be equipped to encourage the Church and spread Your gospel with boldness. Keep me from becoming lukewarm so I will be a light burning brightly for You. Amen.

❧   ❧   ❧

Surrendering all to the Holy Spirit will give us the power we need to be a witness for God, but we must never forget to pray always to God. But what is prayer? How often does God want to hear from us . . .?

FIFTEEN
PRAYER

The Lord hears your prayer
When you call on His name.
He desires your fellowship,
That's why He came.

WHAT IS PRAYER? AND DOES GOD REALLY WANT US TO PRAY?

A Phone Call

Prayer is an active part of a Christian's life. Prayer is a form of communication with God. I think of prayer as a phone call to God. He never hangs up on us. His line is always open, and is never busy. He even paid for the line to be established and has already paid the bill . . .

Another Dime

It seemed everywhere I went I found a dime. When I reached in the dryer to make sure I'd taken out all the clothes, I found a dime.

When I stepped up to board the van, there on the ground, in front of the door, I found a dime. On a windowsill I was dusting, I found a dime. On the floor in my room, I found another dime. In fact, this kept happening for several weeks. It became so frequent to find a solo dime everywhere I turned that I started to suspect it was the whispers of God. Then one day Abigail came running to me with a big smile on her face.

"Mommy! Look what I found!" She lifted her closed fist and opened it palm up to reveal—yes, another dime.

"OK, that's it. Lord what are You trying to say to me, because I sure don't get it!"

The Lord whispered into my heart, "Got a dime? Call someone who cares."

"Ahh, yes," I laughed quietly. "Now I understand," I said, as I smiled and reflected on what that meant. When I was a teen and telephone calls had cost only a dime, the kids had a cruel saying, "Got a dime? Call someone who cares." Of course, it meant that the person saying it didn't care. Usually that message got shortened to, "Gotta dime?" and was immediately understood to be a put-down. But this message from the Lord wasn't cruel—it was sweet and loving. He was letting me know I hadn't been *praying,* as I should. In fact, life had just gotten too busy for anything like that—or so it seemed. The Lord in His goodness was reminding me Who really cares for me. The Lord cares for us and encourages us to tell Him all our cares and our concerns. And as priests, we can pray for others as well. If we're listening, we'll discover times when the Lord will lead us to pray for others, as He did at a church business meeting I attended several years ago . . .

The Church Business Meeting

Arriving late to the church business meeting, I peeked through the doorway and saw my friend waving for me to sit with her in the

front row. I smiled back at her and stood motionless for a few seconds. In my mind I pictured my very pregnant body, which could
no longer walk, but was certain to *waddle* past the entire church to
get to her. I couldn't ignore her welcoming smile, so down the
aisle I waddled and sat quietly beside her. While on the way to sit
with my friend, I noticed some new believers in attendance and
greeted them. I also noticed a tension in the air. Somehow the
word "business" added to the words "church meeting" seems to
cause most of us to take ourselves a little *too* seriously.

I was concerned that these new believers might grow disappointed by the immaturity we older, imperfect believers often dis-
play. I could sense that the Lord was concerned about this, too,
and felt a tugging in my heart urging me to pray for the new believers. As I prayed, I could feel the Holy Spirit guiding me to pray
that these new believers would leave with laughter instead of bad
feelings. For a second, I thought about my request and wondered
how the Lord would be able to accomplish it. But then the issues
under discussion drew my attention back to the meeting.

When the meeting ended, Pastor Rick asked the congregation to
stand and pray. I knew my slip was showing so I remained seated.
But not for long! An elder, whom I love dearly and who is a bit of a
character, loudly asked me why I wasn't standing. Since I was in one
of the dreaded front rows and all eyes quickly focused on me, I decided to rise to my feet and say nothing. This wise decision instantly
turned disastrous. As I stood, smiling at my new, now watchful audience—my slip dropped to the floor. And it didn't fall softly and
gracefully, either! It felt like two angels said, "Ready, set—*pull!*"

For one flashing moment I forgot about my cumbersome pregnant body. I jumped out of the slip, snapped it up off the floor with
one quick sweep and wadded it up with such speed and agility
that I surprised even myself. But I wasn't quick enough. The entire
congregation had seen it all and began laughing uncontrollably.

That is, everyone except for Pastor Rick who, with head bowed was the only obedient person in the room! While everyone roared with laughter, Pastor Rick looked up in confusion. As he looked about the room, he noticed that all eyes still focused on me *and* that I was the only one with a bright red face. He must have known I had done something unusual, but no one could stop laughing long enough to tell him what it was—and *I* certainly wasn't going to tell him!

I'd forgotten all about my earlier prayer . . . until I was walking around Pastor Rick toward the exit. Speaking to the new believers, he said, "I hope the meeting didn't bother you." They all broke into laughter once more when one of the new believers said, "Are you kidding? After what happened to Donna?" At that moment I recognized it was the whispers of the Lord that had led me to pray. The Lord cares so much about people, and if we will listen and pray for them, He will lead us in *how* to pray for them. But don't be too surprised if you become part of the answer to the prayer, too, as I was!

Prayer. It's an open line to a great and mighty God. As we learn to trust in Him more, we learn that we don't need to ever hang up our end of the line either. We can include God in everything we do. That's why the Word says to pray without ceasing. Yet, praying without ceasing used to make me think I needed to say the same thing repeatedly to God—as if He didn't hear me the first time . . .

"God . . . ? God . . . ? God . . . ?"

I have a pet peeve. Repeating my words when I've just said something irritates me. "What?" "Huh?" And other similar responses that require me to restate what I've just said are like fingernails running down a chalkboard to me. Why is this little inconvenience so frustrating? Well, just multiply those irksome words by eight children and one husband, and what might have been a slight imposition soon becomes an irritating annoyance!

Not being heard sends the message to me that I'm not important. I wonder if I have this pet peeve with God as well? Praying and seeking, repeating my requests over and over . . . "God, didn't You hear me the first time I asked? Why must I pray and pray, repeating myself often?" My daughter, Catherine, must have experienced this same frustration with me. When she was younger she would say: "Mom . . . ? Mom . . . ? Mom . . . ?"

Until I finally stopped her verbal barrage by saying, "What?!" She was so preoccupied with her request that she didn't realize I had been listening to her from the moment she first called out to me. Catherine was learning to trust that she's important to me and that I want to hear her needs. I smile as I hear the whispers of the Lord . . . "I'm just like Catherine when calling on You, Lord, aren't I?" My thoughts are so busy with my need that I don't see God not only *hears* me the moment I call out to Him, but *knows* what I need even before I ask Him. God requires that we ask, seek, and knock—and so we will. Then He tells us, ". . . you will call upon Me and go and pray to Me, and I will listen to you. And you will seek Me and find *Me*, when you search for Me with all your heart" (Jeremiah 29:12, 13).

Like Catherine, I'm learning to trust that I'm important to God and that He hears me when I pray. I can even imagine His smile when I keep calling out, "God . . . ? God . . . ? God . . . ?"

I'm reassured by what this Scripture says: "Surely the arm of the Lord is not too short to save, nor his ear too dull to hear" (Isaiah 59:1 NIV). God cares about everything in our lives and hears us when we pray, seeking Him with our whole heart. His arm is not too short to save, either!

My Prayer:

Lord, help me to not only pray to You, but also to hear Your whispers when You call my name. Amen.

❧   ❧   ❧

Prayer is not a one-way communication to God. God desires to speak to us as well. We can learn to recognize His whispers when He does speak. But what are these whispers? To whom will God speak? And when have all Christians heard the whispers of God . . . ?

Sixteen

The Whispers of God

The Lord desires your fellowship,
So He can impart,
The wonder of His mysteries,
Whispered softly to your heart.

WHAT ARE "THE WHISPERS," AND WHO WILL HEAR THEM?

The Quiet Touch From God

The Bible tells an interesting story in 1 Kings, Chapter Nineteen, about a whisper. As the prophet Elijah hid in a cave, waiting to hear from God, a great and strong wind came near. It tore into the mountain around him, breaking rocks into pieces . . . but the Lord wasn't in the wind. Then there was an earthquake . . . but the Lord wasn't in the earthquake. Then there was a fire . . . but the Lord wasn't in the fire. And after the fire there came a gentle *whisper*. When Elijah heard the whisper he recognized it as being God's voice, so he stood at the entrance of the cave and listened. In his time of great need, God spoke to Elijah through a whisper. He could have spoken in a more dramatic method through the strong wind, the earthquake, or the fire, but God chose to speak to Elijah through an intimate *whisper*.

God often whispers into our hearts, yet we need to be like Elijah and recognize His voice. Many times we fail to recognize God's voice because we're looking for the dramatic. God isn't limited in how He speaks to us. He can speak to us through His Word, visions, dreams, visual pictures, other people, natural, and supernatural means.

A well-known example of a time when God used a dramatic method to speak was when He spoke to Moses through a burning bush. If we're looking for our own *burning bush* experience, we'll most likely be disappointed. One reason we may be looking for this type of experience is because we're thinking that God is outside our heart's door—beyond us and unreachable. But God is no longer outside our heart's door knocking. We invited Him in . . . and He dwells within us. So there's no need for the *burning bush* experience—unless God chooses to give us one. God can, of course, speak to us however He pleases. But most often He doesn't use a burning bush to get our attention.

Usually God uses a quiet touch to speak to us. These quiet touches are what I refer to as whispers from God. These whispers are similar to softly spoken whispers in our ear from someone we love. Except God whispers into our heart, not our ears—and what we hear, we receive by faith.

You may ask, "If we see spiritual things dimly, how do we recognize God's whispers?" Recognition happens through relationship. We build relationships by spending time in day-to-day experience with the one we're seeking a relationship with. It's the same with the Lord. By performing our priestly duties and offering up spiritual sacrifices (as mentioned in Chapter Thirteen) such as prayer, worship, reading and obeying the Word, fellowship with other believers, and including the Lord in our daily lives, we develop a relationship with God. Although this relationship helps us to identify God's voice, it's *not* a method to guarantee a constant flow of whispers. God is so infinite and beyond human understanding. No method can increase the amount God speaks to us. But you may still be asking, "Will God speak to *me*?" The answer is, "Absolutely, without a doubt. *Yes!*" In fact, I want to remind you of that special time when God has already spoken to you.

Who Can Hear the Whispers?

Fellowship is the reason God sent His son, not just to give us eternal life, but because, "God *is* faithful, by whom you were called into the fellowship of His Son, Jesus Christ our Lord" (1 Corinthians 1:9).

The Lord calls us to fellowship. Fellowship means companionship and mutual sharing, as in an experience, activity, or interest. Jesus desires our companionship and mutual sharing—our fellowship. Before salvation, Jesus knocked on our heart's door, and now that He's within, this is what He desires to do: "Behold, I stand at the door and knock. If anyone hears My voice and opens the door, I will come in to him and dine with him, and he with Me" (Revelation 3:20).

Dining with the Lord represents our fellowshipping with the Lord, and He with us. The Lord offers fellowship to all who open the door and invite Him into their hearts. Who will hear the whispers of God? *All* who open the door of their hearts, Jesus said: "My sheep hear My voice, and I know them, and they follow Me" (John 10:27).

If you have accepted Jesus as your Lord, you are one of His sheep and He not only will communicate with you in the future— He already has. When you accepted Jesus, the calling of the Lord led you to Him. You may not have realized that you were hearing the whispers of God, but you were. You may say, "But I didn't hear any words in my heart." That's OK, because the whispers aren't always words. We know it was the whispers of God to your heart, because if you responded to the call of salvation you knew you needed Christ in your life. And the only way for you to know that is through the Father calling you, as Jesus said: "No one is able to come to Me unless the Father Who sent Me attracts *and* draws him *and* gives him the desire to come to Me" (John 6:44a AMP).

Yes, God *has* spoken to us . . . But now for a word of caution . . . We need to be careful to test the voice we hear, because there can be problems of misunderstanding and false interpretation. Until we are with Jesus in heaven we'll continue to ask ourselves, "Was that the Lord speaking to me, or the pizza I ate last night?" And this is OK. It's good to question what we've heard, because God's voice is not the only voice our hearts can hear. Satan can deceive us because he appears as a spirit of light, when in fact he is the spirit of darkness. We can also hear our own voice speaking within, and it isn't always easy to tell the difference between the three! And there's still one *other* voice that can sometimes deceive us as well.

Most of us have heard someone who claimed to have heard from God yet said things that didn't agree with what the Word teaches. This can lead us astray and cause us to think that God doesn't speak to us. Because these other voices (including our own) can lead us away from God and the truth we need to deal with them scriptur-ally, i.e., "BELOVED, do not believe every spirit, but test the spirits, whether they are of God" (1 John 4:1a).

To test the whisper we've heard in our heart, we first compare it to what the Word of God says. What we hear will not go against God's Word if it was God's voice speaking it. But how do we make sure we understand the Scriptures as God intended? We can un-derstand by reading the Word as a whole. For example: If there's a Scripture in question, other Scripture will clarify its meaning. More importantly, Jesus gave us a clear promise about Who will teach us truth, "But the Helper, the Holy Spirit, whom the Father will send in My name, He will teach you all things, and bring to your remembrance all things that I said to you" (John 14:26).

We can rely on the Spirit to reveal truth to us. We don't have to fear other voices. Yet I've seen Christians who are so fearful of hearing the false voices they refuse to hear or acknowledge the true whispers of God. This is similar to a person who is so afraid of receiving counterfeit money they refuse to use money at all. Silly. Just as there certainly is counterfeit money, there are counterfeit voices, which can confuse us. But we don't let fake money stop us from shopping! If we're concerned, we test it. It's the same with different voices—if we're in doubt, we test them. More important than trusting money, we trust God. He wants us to recognize His voice by comparing the voices we hear against His own familiar voice. We shouldn't just shut out all voices, because God desires to fellowship (dine) with *all* who open the door of their hearts to His loving Presence.

I know there is one group of people who still may be insisting God won't speak to them, and so they couldn't possibly hear His voice. This group is what I will refer to as "ordinary everyday" people. If you think you might fit into this group, or you know people who do, I have one more whisper story just for you.

The best way to encourage *ordinary everyday* people to recognize the whispers is through the testimony of an ordinary everyday person who *has* heard them. Why is this so important? We'd have a hard time believing a person who's famous, highly educated, possessed of some kind of worldly advantage, or gifted in ministry. If this kind of extraordinary person came to teach us that God speaks to mankind, we'd say, "Yeah, sure, God speaks to you because you're special to God." We humans have a tendency to elevate people with achievements and advantages, but none of these things matter much to God. Hearing the testimony of an ordinary everyday person encourages us that God doesn't favor one person over another. He desires to speak to each of us—even *everyday ordinary* people like ourselves . . .

Ordinary? Who . . . *Me?*

Attending a wonderful writer's conference, I sat next to a man I thought to be of a greater intelligence than myself. As he told me about the book he was working on, I discovered how correct I'd been! This book was about—I couldn't even explain it here correctly. Just trust me that it was way out there, intellectually speaking.

I remember looking straight into Randy's eyes and saying, "That sounds like a very needed book, Randy, but are you making sure that you've written it in such a way that the ordinary everyday person can understand it?"

Randy smiled and sat taller in his chair and answered, "Oh, yes! In fact, I just presented it to a couple of friends of mine to test it, and *they* understood it! She's a home-schooling mother and her husband's a contractor!"

While Randy was still beaming from answering my question so easily, I said rather slowly, "Gee, Randy . . . I think I will go and cry now. You just described me and my husband." Randy said something about excusing himself to remove the remains of his tennis shoes out of his teeth. I smiled at my new friend, knowing God had used him to whisper into my heart. The Lord reminded me that the only way ordinary everyday people would believe this message God placed on my heart—is for them to know and believe that I am an *ordinary everyday* person, too.

Yes, God speaks, and He wants us to recognize His voice so we can respond to and fellowship with Him. This fellowship leads to relationship. The Lord doesn't want us to merely hear His Voice,

He wants *fellowship*, with the ultimate goal of relationship with us. And we don't have to *be* somebody, or *know* somebody, or *do* something, or *earn* something for God to fellowship with us. He not only *will* speak to our hearts in the future—He already has! Be still, and listen . . .

What is God whispering to your heart today . . . ?

Epilogue

"Well, Kevin, it's been several years now since you stood in the door-way of my room. You're a young man heading out for college to become a minister of the Lord. Before you leave home, I need to know if I've I answered your question. Do you recognize God's voice? Oh, to be sure we won't always recognize every touch of God. This would be too much for us. But maybe what's more im-portant than hearing a whisper, is *understanding* that He will speak and that He is close by, and cares for us. Understanding this alone helps us to develop our relationship with God by including Him in every area of our lives. After all, what we're really wanting is to know Him. So tell me, Kevin, have I answered that question of yours that's taken me years to respond . . . ?"

"Yes, Mom, you have done a swell job, because if it wasn't for your answer and encouragement I would probably never be going to a Bible college . . . and I thank you for that."

"Whew! Does this mean I can relax now?" Maybe not—there are five more children still at home, eager to ask me some other perplexing questions!

I hope you've been encouraged to see that God has spoken, does speak, and will again speak to your heart . . . and that we need not *strive* to hear. Just knowing He will lead and guide us in our everyday situation and circumstances is a comfort to the heart—and renders us more open to hear His whispers. God does care. He knows everything about us, and He has a good plan for our life. Hmm . . . That makes me think of another perplexing question: How do we know God's plan (will) for our lives? I guess I really can't relax yet—I'd better get busy writing my next book—
Learning to Know the Will of God.

God bless you!
Donna

Study Guide

These questions and scriptural answers are designed for further study and deeper thought. Study individually or with a group.

Chapter One – Listening As a Child

1. How do we know God desires fellowship with us? 1 Corinthians 1:9

2. Find definitions of fellowship and acquaintance. Define the difference.

3. Explain the difference between someone we have fellowship with, and someone we merely have an acquaintance with? Which relationship does Jesus desire from us?

Chapter Two – Faith to Hear

1. We all have a measure of faith. Romans 12:3

2. What is possible if we use our faith? Mark 9:23

3. Should we see evidence of faith working in our lives? James 2:14–26

Chapter Three – The Spirit Brings Truth

1. What suppresses truth? Romans 1:18

2. The Lord desires truth in our hearts. Psalms 51:6

3. Why will people perish in the end times? 2 Thessalonians 2:9–12

4. How do we teach others the truth? 2 Timothy 2:22–26

Chapter Four – When You Cannot Hear

1. Why is it important to control our thoughts? Matthew 5:27, 28

2. Can we hide our thoughts from God? Hebrews 4:12, 13

3. What did Jesus say about worrying? Matthew 6:25–34

4. What can we do to make certain we hear? Proverbs 1:23 / James 4:7–10

Chapter Five – When Words Have to Be Eaten

1. What is the root problem if our words give death instead of life? Romans 8:5, 6

2. How bad is the tongue (our words)? James 3:2–10

3. What should our conversation be like? Colossians 4:6

4. Will God ever give us the words to speak? Luke 12:12

Chapter Six – His Tender Love

1. Which commandments did Jesus say were the most important? Mark 12:29–31

2. Signs of spiritual growth in a believer. 2 Peter 1:5–8

3. Will great works tell us who the true and false teachers are? Matthew 24:24

4. What will happen if we love our lives more than Jesus? John 12:25

Chapter Seven – God Values Life

1. How does God feel about salvation? 1 Timothy 2:3, 4

2. What name does God call us that reveals His great love for us?
    1 John 3:1

3. God knew us in our mother's wombs. Psalm 139:13–16

4. Raising children. Deuteronomy 6:5–9 / Proverbs 13:24 / Ephesians 6:1–4

Chapter Eight – Broken to Be Made Whole

1. The continual sacrifices of the law could not take away sin, but Jesus took them away once, and for all time. Hebrews 10:1–18

2. Our works alone cannot save us. Ephesians 2:8, 9

3. Our new covenant (contract) with God. Jeremiah 31:31–34

Chapter Nine – A Matter of Security

1. We're tested as gold and silver – God calls us His people. Zechariah 13:9

2. How should we respond to trials in our life? And why? 1 Peter 4:12–19

3. We're not anything by ourselves, our sufficiency is in God. 2 Corinthians 3:5

Chapter Ten – God's Defenses Against Sin

1. Shall we sin because we're not under the law but under grace? Romans 6

2. How do we prepare ourselves for Jesus? 1 Thessalonians 5:21–24

3. We'll know more clearly what is right and wrong as we mature. Hebrews 5:14

Chapter Eleven – No Longer In Alcatraz

1. We are a slave to one of these or the other. Romans 6:16

2. What do the Scriptures say about people who lack self-control? Proverbs 25:28

3. How to build each other up. 1 Thessalonians 5:11–15

4. Be alert (awake), because we have an adversary, the devil. 1 Peter 5:8, 9

5. Jesus tells us to not rejoice in our power over devils, but ... Luke 10:17–20

Chapter Twelve – Keeping the Candle Burning

1. If we sleep at harvest time, we'll cause ourselves shame. Proverbs 10:5

2. How do we walk as children of the Light? Ephesians 5:8–21

3. We can reflect the glory of God. 2 Corinthians 3:18

4. What do we need to do for fellowship with each other and God? 1 John 1:7

Chapter Thirteen – Our Priestly Duties

1. We're no longer separated from God. Hebrews 10:16–22

2. We're the temple. 1 Corinthians 3:16

3. Which does God prefer: sacrifices or obeying? 1 Samuel 15:22, 23

4. God promises to teach each of us. 1 John 2:27

Chapter Fourteen – Total Surrender

1. Spirit's baptism promised by Jesus. Luke 24:49

2. Gifts of the Holy Spirit operating even in the end times. Joel 2:28, 29

3. Baptism gives boldness to witness. Acts 1:8; 4:31

4. Study the Spirit's baptism in 1 Corinthians, chapters 12–14.

5. Examples of the baptism can be found in the book of Acts.

Chapter Fifteen – Prayer

1. Christ tells us how to pray. Matthew 6:5–13

2. Example of a prayer from a righteous man. James 5:16–18

3. Can we pray for a nation? What good could it do? 2 Chronicles 7:14

4. The Lord delights in our prayers. Proverbs 15:8

Chapter Sixteen – The Whispers of God

1. Will we always "hear" or understand spiritual things clearly? 1 Corinthians 13:12

2. Jesus calls us friends. John 15:15

3. The test of knowing Jesus. 1 John 2:3–5

4. The Lord will direct us. Isaiah 30:21

5. Who did Jesus say would hear His voice? John 18:37

Do you have a manuscript hidden in your closet or burning in your heart?

It has been said that because this is the age of computers and word processors that *everyone* sees themselves as a writer. Instead of being discouraged that your works will have less value because there is a flood of written work available, listen to the Lord's voice. Has He called you to write? If so, do it. You may not be accepted by the major publishing houses on the first call—or ever. However, that isn't why we write.

Don't be discouraged if your manuscript isn't picked up by the "big" guys (they're good guys, too). It may not be the route God has called you to take. My agent shopped my manuscript around to many different houses—for a few years. I received many positive responses including one from a well-known publisher that said, "This book has a lovely Guidepost feel." Yet, instead of feeling discouraged by being ultimately rejected, I realized that—yes . . . this book needs to be in print. I found that I was actually encouraged from these rejections and discovered, after traveling the "normal" route of trying to be published—there really were alternatives.

After spending several months of looking, learning, pricing, evaluating products, procedure, and just looking for plain old godly integrity in a publishing company . . . I discovered the perfect fit . . . WinePress Publishing. I further discovered that they not only have what it takes to get a book in print—professionally, they have everything I was looking for—and more!

If God has given you a message to write, don't let it collect dust in your closet, or weigh heavily on your heart any longer—call WinePress, and see if they will be the perfect fit for you. Remember, our faith is not in ourselves, or even in our abilities—it is in God alone. If God placed a message on your heart to give to others . . . do it! You'll be blessed to see His hand move because . . . He delights in making the foolish things of this world confound the wise!

In Him and His Love,
Donna Fitzpatrick

800-326-4674
info@winepresspub.com
www.winepresspub.com

To order additional copies of

LEARNING TO HEAR

THE
WHISPERS
OF GOD

Have your credit card ready and call

Toll free: (877) 421-READ (7323)

or send $11.99 each plus $4.95 S&H*

to

WinePress Publishing
PO Box 428
Enumclaw, WA 98022

www.winepresspub.com

*WA residents, add 8.6% sales tax

* Add $1.00 S&H for each additional book ordered.